Camillus, Halfway There

Dr. David Beebe

Library of Congress Copyright Office - April 2008

"Camillus, Halfway There" by Dr. David Beebe - Publisher

ISBN 978-1-60643-381-2

Printed by: Syracuse Lithographing Co.

Book design by Kathleen Miles

Dedication

This is very easy.

For most of my life, I have been planning to create a book and dedicate it to my wife, Liz.

She has tried to guide me in many ways, and there is a good reason that many in our canal group call her "Saint Liz."

Liz, with your love and friendship, anything is possible.

Appreciation

We would like to express our deepest appreciation and thanks for the many people that have supported and helped in completing this project.

We would like to thank Tom Grasso in writing the chapter on the Geology of this region and being a friend to us for many years. He is an inspiration to all of us.

For the assistance of Craig Williams whose immeasurable knowledge of the canals of New York State made this book possible. He is a national treasure and his recall and guidance is a challenge to all of us.

A special thanks to Fenton Hanchett who contributed many fine drawings and shared his engineering knowledge.

To Lee Hidy who read the manuscript and made corrections in the use of the English language.

To Russ Donahue, who introduced the chapters with opening sentences .

To Mike Riley who is always looking ahead with excellent ideas .

To Gerri Wright for her advice and encouragement.

To Amy O'Shea who always seeks answers to all canal questions.

A special thanks to all the members of our close canal group who helped to create a unique canal park which other groups have modeled .

Introduction

Today, there is more interest and understanding on the subject of canals. I had an experience that reflects this increased enthusiasm today which was not present 20 years ago. In 1980 I visited Waterloo, New York looking for a canal site. I knew I was close to this location, but nothing was familiar. I noticed a man in his mid-twenties exiting from a youth center, and I jumped out of my truck to ask for his assistance. His answer was loud and clear! "Hey, I only know baseball!" I said, "thank you", and found the site a short time later.

There is a second incident that shows the obscurity of the canal in the late 1970's. One morning, when I arrived at Sims' Museum, I noticed a middle-aged gentleman walking in our parking lot. I parked my truck, and I approached the man and asked, "May I help you?" He answered, "Can you tell me where the canal is located?" I said politely, that if he were to turn around, he would see the canal 20 feet away!

The Town of Camillus attained a very special and unique place in the history of the Erie Canal in New York State. Richard Wright was the first person that I am aware of to have observed and stated a very special designation for the Town of Camillus. Dick Wright was instrumental in founding the Canal Society of New York State in Buffalo, New York on Saturday, October 13, 1956, during the closing hours of the annual meeting of the New York State Historical Association. He was elected secretary-treasurer of the organization and DeWitt Clinton of Buffalo, a great, great grandson of the governor, was president. Dick Wright was the long time Director of the Onondaga Historical Society on Montgomery Street in Syracuse, New York.

It is interesting to note that a photo of the Nine Mile Creek aqueduct was featured on page 3 of our Canal Society publication "Bottoming Out" (Vol. 1, No. 2, Jan. 1957) and stated that the Aqueduct was the sixth longest on the Erie Canal.

Dick wrote on Plate 57-25, volume 7 of the Enlargement of the Erie Canal by Van R. Richmond, State Engineer and Surveyor, 1871, the following.

"Halfway point on the Enlarged Canal was 838 feet West of Br. # 113." Bridge #113 was the Camillus Bridge over the First Enlargement Canal , which was a highway and change bridge for the Nine Mile Creek Feeder.

Dick Wright computed the following:

351.4/2 = 175.7 miles (total length of canal divided by 2)

1855431.4/2 = 927715.7 (measured in feet from Albany)

Br. # 113 926878 (midpoint measured from bridge #113)

837.7 (exact midpoint of canal west in feet west of Camillus bridge #113) [1]

In summary - the exact mid-point of the First Enlargement, between Buffalo and Albany, was located 838 feet to the west of Devoe Road. We have erected a sign at this exact location on the berme (side of canal opposite the towpath) side of the canal.

Nine Mile Creek plays an extremely important role in the Camillus area and contributed to the success of watering the Erie Canal. How did Nine Mile Creek get its name? It would be logical to note that since the Creek originates at the outflow of Otisco Lake and flows basically North into Onondaga Lake, the length of the Creek should be nine miles. Not so. The Creek is longer than nine miles. The following statements are written in Onondaga's Centennial, Vol. 1, 1896. "This is the only stream of note in the town. It was so named from the fact that it was nine miles from Onondaga Hollow on the east and the same distance from Josiah Buck's on the west."

This is not a chronology of the history of the canals. There have been many fine books and articles written on the canal history.

This book may be considered a limited 'nitch' book concentrating in the Camillus area. This is not entirely true. The Town of Camillus Erie Canal Park has one of each type of structure erected on both the Grand Canal (Clinton's Ditch) and The First Enlargement . The structures are prototypes, and we will attempt to describe how they were constructed and how they functioned. We hope by this comparison, a person can determine how all of the canal structures function within the New York State canal system.

I do expect and encourage differences of opinion and interpretation when reading this book. Please write to me stating errors or adding additional facts. There isn't a book written that can encompass all of the facets of the tremendously large subject of the New York canal.

Photography is an extremely important side activity which documents the progress and activities in our Canal Park. Photos are used extensively in the Museum to depict the many facets of the canals. Liz and I visit Cape Cod often. On several trips, we photographed the seals and whales even in the winter time. I purchased electric socks for my wife, Liz, so that her feet would not freeze in the zero degree

[1] Possible error in calculation of length at slip at Buffalo 15 feet max. would make 830 feet above. (Dick Wright)

temperatures that we encounter on Cape Cod in February. A choice had to be made, however. My camera was not functioning properly due to the low temperatures. I used one of the electric socks to warm the camera while taking photos of the seals. At least Liz still had one sock to warm one foot! What more could you want? I have a very understanding wife! [2]

Note: CSNYS is the Canal Society of New York State.

GEOLOGY OF THE REGION

The 19th-century Erie Canals and the Barge Canal in the canalized Seneca River are located over a weak belt of shale several miles wide known as the Salina Group. It was deposited approximately 400 million years ago (Late Silurian Period) in very shallow, often hypersaline waters in an arid climate. The result is a curious package of shales and dolostones totaling nearly 1,000 feet in thickness and containing deposits of evaporites such as salt and gypsum.

In the Pleistocene Epoch or the Ice Age, four glacial stages are generally recognized, separated by relatively long periods (200,000 years) of warm interglacial ice-free stages. The last glacier to effect the region is known as the Wisconsin stage and it melted back past the study area approximately 10,000 or 12,000 years ago. The front of the ice (melting edge) would occasionally readvance over recently deposited glacial materials. In this way, the streamlined glacially-molded hills known as drumlins were formed. Many of the hills from Rochester to Syracuse are drumlins.

In front of the ice sheet, high level lakes were imponded between the ice and the highlands to the south. These lakes are called proglacial lakes and as the ice melted northward, their levels dropped. Montezuma Marsh is the last remnant of glacial Lake Iroquois that was so widespread in the Lake Ontario basin. Since the ice acted as a dam and the Thousand Island outlet was still covered by ice these lakes escaped generally, but not always, eastward to the Mohawk Valley. The escaping lake water comingled with other meltwaters and carved wide, relatively flat bottomed, valleys aligned more or less in an east-west direction called meltwater channels.

West of Syracuse, the 19th-century Erie Canals followed a series of east-west trending glacial melt water channels (valleys) south of the Seneca River and at a higher elevation. The channel from Memphis to Camillus is especially striking. These valleys are poorly drained and commonly contain swamps, many of which contain beds of marl. Therefore, Clinton's Ditch hugged the winding sides of the valleys, mostly along

---

[2] All of the prints labeled OHA were purchased from the Onondaga Historical Association and printed with permission as long as credit was assigned to OHA. A letter has been sent notifying the OHA that a book is in preparation which will contain OHA photos of the Camillus area and a use fee was paid.

higher ground composed of glacial sands and gravel. This original Erie skirted the south edge of the swamps throughout most of the Jordan Level and, therefore, the prism is visible along the Canal Road east of Memphis and the Peru Road from Jordan to Peru.

In opting for this route through central Onondaga County, the canal commissioners were forced into a short summit level by this geography. This bump on the canal's profile would be a defining characteristic of the Erie Canal in this western part of the county. To the west of Jordan and to the east of Camillus, it all went downhill. The corollary to this summit level was that enough water had to pour into the level to maintain navigable conditions. Water was constantly lost by lockages to the east and west. Trying to find enough water here plagued the State's canal officials as it also did on the more famous summit level to the east, the Rome Summit.

It did not have to be this way. The first major navigable route in central New York was to the north, on the Seneca River. Throughout the colonial era and in the early part of the 19th century, boaters primarily used the Seneca to reach the interior. With good reason, Dr. Baldwin established his canal along this waterway. When James Geddes launched his exploration in 1808 for what eventually becomes the Erie Canal, the assumption was that the Seneca River would continue to be used. The practicality of an "artificial river" further inland, however, was soon demonstrated.

The geology review of this region was reprinted by permission from the author, Dr. Thomas Grasso, President of the Canal Society of the State of New York.

Contents

Chapter 1

Camillus Erie Canal Park

As my wife and I saw trucks continually filling the First Enlargement with trash in the early 1970's and moving closer to the Warners-Amboy Road, we asked the Town of Camillus if we could save the historic canal for recreational purposes. With my Audubon background the Supervisor asked me if I would head the committee. What was my canal background ? The answer was zero .The Camillus Erie Canal Park was established in 1972 when we obtained 164 acres from the State of New York for the sum of $15 per acre.

We were on the way!

No one had any idea of the impact nor envisioned the park that we have today. The Camillus Town Board authorized $100.00 for our budget the first year. With a gift from the Jaycees we put up telephone pole gates, still visible, to keep the integrity of the park. Then the volunteers cleared the canal bed of trees and undergrowth. Dams were constructed. Buildings, bridges, and docks appeared. Trails were established. We soon discovered that within our seven mile linear canal park we had all the components necessary to operate a canal: Gere Lock, the 1844 Nine Mile Creek Aqueduct, a feeder, portions of the original Erie Canal and First Enlargement and Culvert 59. We constructed replicas of a lock tender's shanty and Sims' Store Museum. In chapter 5 I will go into more detail about the Nine Mile Creek Aqueduct, listed on the National Registry of Historical Places. We plan to go to bid in 2008 to restore the Aqueduct. Of the original 32 aqueducts, it will be the ONLY restored, navigable aqueduct in New York State. The estimated cost is $2,225,000.

The key word is restored. Our Nine Mile Creek Aqueduct is on the National Registry of Historical Places, and we are required by the New York State Office of Parks, Recreation and Historic Preservation (OPRHP) to restore our Aqueduct as close to the original plans as possible. The Aqueducts at Chittenango Creek and Cowassalon Creek were poured full width in concrete. These Aqueducts would be navigable, but the trunk carrying water were not restored in wood and certainly not close to the original plans.

In addition we have 13 miles of nature trails , and we discovered that it could be the setting for more than 50 activities such as hiking, biking, kayaking , cross country skiing and snow mobiling. One of these trails goes to the Dill's Pond area. We worked every Saturday for 12 months to complete this project. The work continued in the winter with the temperature being 3 degrees below zero on several occasions. We have a group of dedicated volunteers.

In 1996 the Camillus Canal Society was established to raise funds for the Aqueduct Restoration Project. The mission of the park is to preserve the artifacts and structures of the towpath era: to educate people about the importance of historic canals and provide a unique recreational area within the Town of Camillus. The Camillus Erie Canal Park works within the Town of Camillus Parks and Recreation Department. The town provides the park a budget for its operation and maintenance.

In 2007, the park encompasses over 420 acres. We are a site for Earth Day, Days of Caring, Crop Walks, folksmarch, scouting events and Eagle Scout Projects.

We have an active school program and provide nearly 200 interpretive programs for 1700 school children . Today we are a part of the National Heritage Corridor. We are an important link of the Canal Way Trail from Albany to Buffalo. We are neighbors to the Camillus Forest Unique Area and Nine Mile Creek Water Trail. The outgrowth of what has been done in Camillus, strictly by volunteers, has served as model for many small towns along the canal.

The volunteers do the impossible! We have Saturday 'work parties' the year around, and during our summer season, May through October, we have a 40 minute guided boat tour on the historic canal which includes a brief stop at the beautiful 1844 Nine Mile Creek Aqueduct.

SIMS' STORE *(front view)* Photos of Sims' Store were presented to our Museum by the former Richard Wright from the OHA collection.

SIMS' STORE (rear view) OHA photo

SIMS' STORE Photo from the Onondaga Historical Association of the Original Sims' Store on the Warners Amboy Road (now Route 173) Looking south-east. Sims' store and barn bridge on right. OHA

WEED CUTTER - Bill Winks on the cutter.

THE OTISCO serves as our dinner cruise and tour boat. The dinner cruise gang put up with high water, low water and no water. This boat was built by the canal volunteers and is scheduled to be replaced with a pontoon boat powered by twin electric outboard motors in 2008.

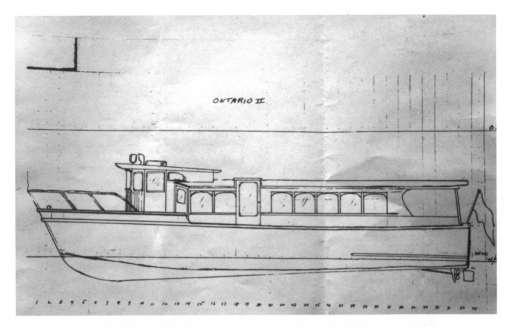

ONTARIO II - Sketch by John Settineri

Ontario being moved through ice on the canal.

Ontario - 2002
Taken in front of Sims'
Store Museum - author.

Our Camillus Parks and Recreation Department installed a chain link gate at Gere Lock to discourage dumping. Once the gate was installed, they placed a small chain to secure the gate with their own padlock. One evening, I visited the lock to cut a link out of the chain on the gate and to place our own canal padlock. With this method, we do not have to make duplicate keys and the various departments each have their own padlock. I had just cut the chain with a hacksaw, and I felt the presence of something behind me. I turned and just inches behind me was a Camillus police cruiser. He had drifted in quietly to catch a person red-handed cutting the town chain. I looked down at him and said, "You are probably wondering what I am doing?" The officer looked up at me and said that he believed that he recognized me. I explained what I was doing, and I felt much better!

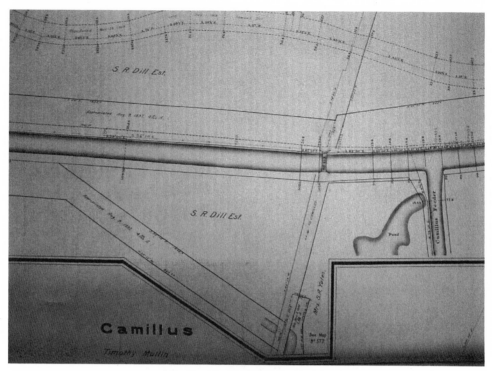

Schillner map - 1896 Shows the canal First Enlargement and the Camillus Road bridge # 113. The Camillus Feeder is shown in the lower right and the top dotted line shows the route of the Clinton's Ditch 1820 canal. - *NYS Archives*

Pile driving in front of the present day Sims' Museum and the feeder exit - OHA Looking south-east

CAMILLUS ROAD CHANGE BRIDGE (now Devoe Road) - from the collection of Jane Maxwell by permission - was considered a trapezoidal, wood highway and change bridge. Tow-lines were dropped allowing canal boats to drift into the feeder. The mules left the towpath, crossed over the bridge, and the tow-lines were reattached in the feeder. The boats would be towed into the Village of Camillus.

Camillus Road Bridge showing old berme abutment - 318C

'L' shaped limestone block used on the ends of the farm and change bridges to support the curve of the bridge - from the Amboy bridge

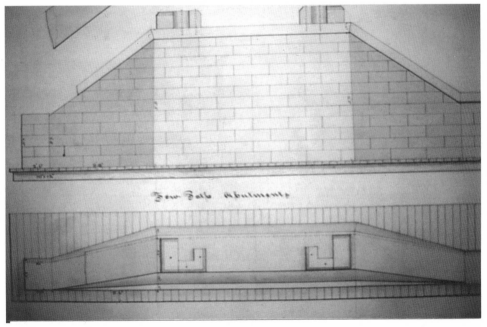

A plan showing the position of the 'L' shaped support stone

    a. The top portion of the photo shows the 'L' shaped support stones on the top of the coping stones.

    b. The bottom portion is a superior view clearly showing the 'L' shaped support stones. NYS Archives

A farm bridge on a smaller scale was constructed behind the Sims' Museum.

Camillus feeder in foreground - laying stone on towpath slope wall - Camillus Bridge over first enlargement in background - OHA

Camillus feeder on right - Taken from Camillus bridge, looking east. 45G OHA

New vertical towpath wall west of Camillus aqueduct. February 28, 1898. 378C OHA

Photo showing excavation of prism, puddling and laying slope wall. Sta. 173 31A 2500 feet west of Camillus aqueduct. OHA

A Steam Engine exhibit has been established within our Erie Canal Park. The exhibit houses a 1918, 450 H.P. Corliss type simple single cylinder steam engine with an 11 1/2 foot, seven ton flywheel. The steam engine was donated to the Camillus Canal Society in 1998 and rescued from the now demolished Midtown Plaza in Downtown Syracuse, New York. The engine formerly served the L.C. Smith Typewriter Company. It is an excellent example of the Corliss-type mill engines which powered industry in the late 19th Century and early 20th Centuries.

In the Village of Camillus, there was a walkway between the buildings on the south side of Main Street. In this walkway, or ally, there was a poster advertising the Barnum and Bailey Circus that was coming to town. Years passed and the ally was incorporated as part of the buildings and became Murphy's Restaurant and bar in the mid-1990's. When the restaurant was remodeled, they uncovered this poster in all of its vivid colors.

Interior of steam engine exhibit showing 11 foot flywheel - 2003

Saving and preserving artifacts is extremely important as they are disappearing very fast into private collections or landfills. Our CSNYS collection of canal iron was collected by its members prior to their removal or destruction. I had noticed a twenty foot control rod lying in Skaneateles Creek in Jordan, New York. This had been a part of the control gate allowing water to flow into the canal or remain in Skaneateles Creek.

On a Sunday morning, I removed the rod with difficulty and proceeded to walk back to my car. The rod was heavier than I had expected, weighing in the neighborhood of 60 pounds. I balanced the rod on my shoulder and walked through the Village of Jordan. I approached a church exactly as they were letting out. I found about 25 to 30 people in front of me. I said, "good morning" and "hello," and two young men offered to help me carry the load to my vehicle. I replied, "Thank you very much, but I have it balanced on my shoulder." The control rod now resides in our Camillus museum collection safe for the future.

Barnum and Bailey Circus poster - photo by author

Cole Brothers Circus poster - Black Smith Shop at CSNYS Erie House, Port Byron, New York - photo by author

A second poster from the Cole Brother's Circus was located in the building owned by the CSNYS in Port Byron. A wood work shop was at one end and the other end of the building housed a three stall mule barn used during the canal first enlargement.

The stalls in the mule barn in Port Byron - CSNYS   Erie House - photo by author

Millionaire contractor, "Sim' Dunfee", clowning with a workman near Camillus in the late 1890's - CSNYS

An unusual team on the towpath near Camillus. Sunday pleasure boaters who ran out of gas. - CSNYS

The crew who built and repaired boats at Bert Riley's boatyard in Buffalo. - CSNYS

The previous three photos, with their original captions, were exhibited on the Erie Maid in 1967. The floating exhibit was sponsored by the State's Council on the Arts celebrating the ground breaking for the Grand Canal in Rome, New York on July 4, 1817. The boat traveled 931 miles on the Barge Canal and was a two-decked quarter boat propelled by a tug boat.

A quarter boat similar to the Erie Maid at Barge Canal Albion terminal in 2001.

Chapter 2

Digging the Original Canal – Clinton's Ditch

The Erie Canal came into being through the efforts of a few visionary men at the beginning of the 19th Century.

Judge Joshua Forman, from the Town of Onondaga, was the first person to propose the Erie Canal project to the State Legislature. He offered a resolution to the Assembly, February 4, 1808 appointing a joint committee to take into consideration the propriety of exploring and causing an accurate survey to be made of the most eligible route for a canal from the tide-waters of the Hudson to Lake Erie. To that end, the Congress might be enabled to appropriate such sums necessary to the accomplishment of that great national object. (Assembly Doc. Jan.23, 1863, p. 95)

Joshua Forman is buried in Oakwood Cemetery in Syracuse, New York. There is an excellent description of his work accomplished on the canal on his burial vault which reads as follows:

"FOUNDER OF THE CITY OF SYRACUSE, AUTHOR OF THE SAFETY FUND BANKING LAW OF THIS STATE, THE FIRST PERSON WHO OFFERED A RESOLUTION IN THE LEGISLATURE AND PROCURED AN APPROPRIATION FOR THE CONSTRUCTION OF THE ERIE CANAL. HE WAS BORN AT PLEASANT VALLEY IN THE COUNTY OF DUCHESS N.Y. ON THE 6TH DAY OF SEPTEMBER 1777, AND DIED AT RUTHERFORDTON N.C. ON THE 4TH DAY OF AUGUST 1849"

Forman-Levenworth Mausoleum - author

Joshua Forman's tombstone inscription - author

Inscription inside mausoleum - author

Joshua Forman was one of the first six toll collectors appointed on the Erie Canal. His salary was $250.00. Tolls were first levied on the Erie canal, July 1st, 1820, and the amount received in that year from tolls was $5,244. (Assembly, 1863, p.112)

On March 21, 1808, a resolution was offered directing the Surveyor General to accomplish an accurate survey. It was adopted in the Assembly, but was postponed in the Senate until April 6th when it passed by a vote of 20 to 9. Six hundred dollars was appropriated to defray the survey expenses. James Geddes was the first engineer appointed by the Surveyor General, Simeon DeWitt, June 11, 1808. DeWitt Clinton was chosen President of the Board of Canal Commissioners. The Commissioners made application to Congress for aid. This was not forth coming as Congress had backed a non-profitable canal to the east. Transportation from Buffalo to New York City was $100.00 per ton to ship. After the canal was completed, DeWitt Clinton estimated that it would cost $10.00 to transport a ton of cargo. (Assembly 1863- p. 104)

Money was borrowed on the credit of the State as the Federal Government thought the canal was a poor investment. The canal was started at Rome, July 4th, 1817. DeWitt Clinton was born in 1769 and was a two time Governor of the State of New York from 1817 to 1823 and from 1825 to 1828. He died February 11, 1828 and is buried in Green Wood Cemetery in Brooklyn, New York.

I would like to go back and describe the origins of the Original canal (Clinton's Ditch) as described in the Laws of the State of New York ,Volume 1, in 1825.

In the index under Canal Eras, on June 17, 1817, the first contract was made with individuals to commence the work in making the Canal under the law of April 15, 1817. On July 4th, 1817, the first excavation began. It was noted , that on that day, 58 miles was contracted and 15 miles of canal was considered completed.

From August 10 to December 10, 1818, between two and three thousand men, with half as many horses and cattle, and a great variety of mechanical inventions "unremittingly" were employed in the construction of the canal. From January 31, 1818, to the succeeding season (in 1819), 117 miles of the canal was completed.

In 1819, the whole middle section of the Clinton's Ditch (96 miles in length) was completed by October, including the lateral canal at Salina. This was located in the Regional Market area along Park Street north of Syracuse.

In 1819, it was noted that villages were rapidly rising on the borders of the canal. On October 23, 1819, the canal was opened with great ceremony, and navigated by the canal commissioners from Utica to Rome. It should be noted that in two years and five months, 120 miles of canal navigation were completed. The average expense per mile, of 96 miles, which includes the entire length of the middle section, was $11,792.00.

Asa Broadwell was the contractor of the lock-aqueduct at Nine-Mile Creek. (p. 342 Canal Laws) The prices given for the masonry of the locks, inclusive of stone-cutting is three dollars per perch of 16 1/2 solid feet. The one exception in one case, where $8 per perch is given for the first foot solid measure, on the inside face of the walls, and $1.50 per perch for the residue of the lock-walls. (p. 342 Canal Laws) A perch is defined as a solid measure for stone, commonly 16 1/2 by 1 1/2 feet by 1 foot.

Digging the Original Canal - Clinton's Ditch

One of the major problems of digging a canal in 1817 was the wetness of the soil in the Camillus - Jordan summit level. In Canal Laws there is a description of the deep cutting through the marl meadow in the Town of Camillus. "The summit level extended from the Nine-Mile creek to the Skaneateles outlet, a distance of between eleven and twelve miles, and involving the construction of two additional locks, of eleven feet lift each, but relieving the line from all the difficulties of the marl meadow" (p. 401 Canal Laws - Vol. i)

Canal Laws are a two volume set of the Laws of the State of New York in relation to the Erie and Champlain Canals together with the annual reports of the Canal Commissioners and other documents. They also contained correct maps, delineating the routes of the Erie and Champlain Canals, and designating the lands through which they pass. The two volumes were published as official documents relating to the Erie and Champlain Canals, February 8, 1825 in Albany, by Authority of the State, E. and E. Hosford, printers.

"Because, at the Nine-Mile creek, it admits of the substitution of stone arches, in the aqueduct, instead of a wood trunk; and at the Skaneateles, of an entire stone aqueduct, in place of a dam with guard locks. At both of these places, excellent stone are contracted for, at reasonable prices." "A very few of the contractors are foreigners, who have recently arrived in this country; but far the greatest part of them are native farmers, mechanics, merchants and professional men, residing in the vicinity of the line; and three - fourths of all the laborers were born among us."

Laying concrete at Station 180, 3200 feet west of the Camillus Aqueduct 327C Note the riprap on sides of the prism and bottom support timber. The prism is defined on the improved plans of the Enlarged Erie in 1848 in the middle division as 70 feet across the canal at the water line and 52.5 feet at the bottom with a water depth of 7 feet. OHA #25

As noted, the Irish, which were extremely prominent in digging the Enlarged Erie (1836 - 1862), played a small role in digging the earlier Clinton's Ditch.

Machinery was used for grubbing and clearing. The endless screw was one piece of machinery. The screw was connected with a roller, a cable, a wheel and a crank enabling one man to fell a tree of considerable size without any cutting about its roots.

The endless screw is mounted in a strong frame of wood and iron fastened to the ground approximately 100 feet from the foot of the tree. The cable runs from the screw around the trunk of the tree 50 or 60 feet from the ground. The crank is turned, moving the screw winding the cable on the roller and wheel. The tree is eventually

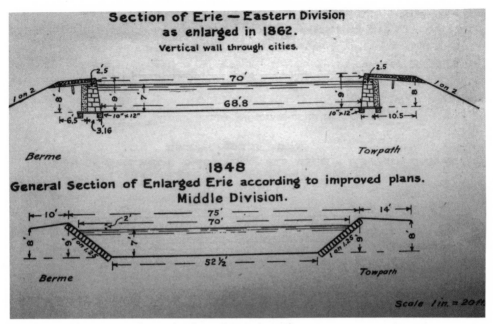

Section of Erie — Eastern Division
as enlarged in 1862.
Vertical wall through cities.

1848
General Section of Enlarged Erie according to improved plans.
Middle Division.

Scale 1 in. = 20 ft.

Photo showing prism with a scale of 1 inch equals 20 feet.

pulled down toward the anchored endless screw. Similar endless screws are used to raise water from a stream into irrigation ditches. Grubbing is defined as to dig, clear of roots and stumps - to dig up by the roots. Another method of clearing the land is using a narrow plow to cut smaller roots up to two inches in diameter. Two oxen were used.

An easier method was also introduced in the 1817 time era. The stump puller consisted of two strong wheels, 16 feet in diameter and connected together by a round axle-tree, 20 inches thick and 30 inches long. Another wheel 14 feet in diameter is placed between the outer wheels, but allowed to rotate on the axle-tree. The apparatus is moved so that the tree stump (The tree is cut down leaving 3 to 4 feet of stump) to be pulled is under the axle-tree behind the middle wheel. The outer wheels are braced so they will not move. A very strong chain is hooked around the stump and over the middle rotating wheel to a team of oxen or horses. The stump is pulled from the earth.

The expense of the wheel, axle-tree, chain and rope is about $250. Seven workers and a pair of horses can grub 30 to 40 large stumps in a day. Large stumps may require four horses

Quicksand was avoided in the Camillus - Jordan summit level by placing the canal prism higher on a hillside and thus avoiding the quicksand. This caused the Clinton's Ditch prism to be very serpentine in its path. The First Enlargement in this area (1845) straightened out the Ditch and placed the prism eleven feet lower than the Clinton's Ditch and directly through the quicksand areas, especially in the Warners area. We will discuss the stabilization of the sides and bottom of the canal in a later chapter.

Model of stump puller by Fenton Hanchett.

Old scrapper restored - author

Scrapers - wooden scrapers with metal wrought iron edges and runners were used to scoop out soil and pile it onto the towpath and berme banks. The operator would raise the handles of the scoop causing the leading edge to bite into the soil. He would then lower his arms when the scoop was full and when ready, would raise and throw the handles over the scoop thus emptying the soil.

Picks and shovels were used with wheelbarrows made in Jordan, New York. The present Bennett Bolt Works, Inc. is the same building that produced wheelbarrows starting in 1815.

Photo showing mule pulling scraper.

Photo of new metal scraper.

Wheel-barrow from Sim's

Camillus Ditch Aqueduct and Lock

Asa Broadwell was the contractor for the Ditch Lock and aqueduct. He signed the contract on February 5, 1819, and Myron Holley also signed on behalf of the Canal Commissioners. Asa Broadwell agreed to perform and construct in the most substantial and workman like manner the lock with a eleven foot lift and the 120 foot stone arch aqueduct. The lock walls were constructed within the south wing walls of the aqueduct for lateral support. The contract stated that the said lock and aqueduct shall be laid in mortar well tempered and worked and the walls shall be thoroughly grouted. The two structures were constantly inspected by the engineer, Benjamin Wright. The contract refers to Asa Broadwell by his first name Asa.

We have located in the center of Nine Mile Creek the arch support for the middle of Clinton's Ditch aqueduct. In the month of July 1834, the stone aqueduct at Nine Mile creek, commenced leaking excessively through one of its arches, and it was anticipated that such a breach would occur, as to interrupt navigation. Piles were driven in the bed of the creek, to support heavy braces of timber placed against the sides of the arches to prevent them from falling. This aqueduct will also require to be rebuilt within a short time. (CCR Assembly. Doc, 1835) The wooden support posts are located today below the waterfall. When we kayak, the paddler must stay to the left side of the rapids to avoid the posts.

"The following is from Canal Commissioner's Report Assembly. Doc. 60, 1840.

The masonry in the abutments, pier and arches, has given such indications of failing, as to require the placing of long timber braces against EACH side of the aqueduct. (author's italics) The lock adjoining the aqueduct has been repaired: also the lock tender's house.

The aqueduct over the Nine Mile creek has required additional bracing and repairing to continue it in use through the season of navigation. The new line of the canal will be brought into use in the spring (of 1845), and this aqueduct will not be required for purposes of navigation. (CCR Assembly. Doc. 28, 1845)"

Mr. and Mrs. Thompson who lived on the farm adjacent to the lock lot, remembered people going down the first enlargement towpath from Route 173 and removing the ditch lock stones for personal use. We believe that the base support stones may still line the lock. We excavated the composite miter sill a few years ago for location purposes. The composite miter sill supported a wooden sill that acted as a seal on the bottom of the miter gates.

A valuable description of our Camillus Aqueduct appears on p. 350 in the Canal Commissioner's report of the Public Documents related to New York Canals, February 1820. "The Aqueduct over Nine-Mile creek was originally intended to consist of stone abutments and piers with a wood trunk. It is constructed exclusively of stone and has been much enlarged by raising the level of the canal eleven feet." "Nine-Mile creek is crossed by a stone aqueduct of two arches, 30 feet chord, which is attached to the lock. A new location for the Jordan level was later proposed the two ditch locks will be dispensed with." (Annual C.C. report - no. 65 - 1835 , p. 138) Many Ditch crossings used dams and slack-water navigation with guard locks. There were 83 lift locks with some records showing 84 lift locks. Stone was used in each lock with each lock measuring 90 feet by 15 feet. Boats capable of carrying 75 tons of cargo were used on this canal.

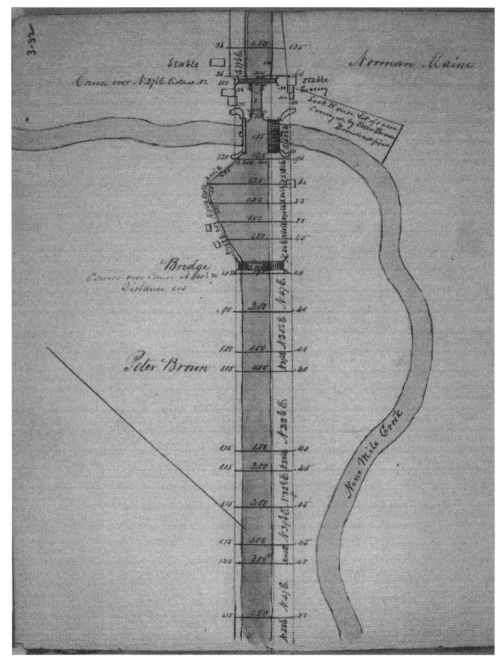

Ditch Map - Holmes Hutchinson 1834

The 120 foot Aqueduct northern abutment consisting of wing-walls and prism, lies on the south edge of the present Thompson farm. This is the only remaining aqueduct abutment in existence in New York State. This valuable site was never abandoned by the State of New York and never sold. The only remaining arch (originally consisted of four arches) of the original 18 Ditch aqueducts exists under the St. John's Church parking lot in Port Byron, New York.

I was walking through a person's back yard in Port Byron to obtain a better camera angle of the only surviving Clinton's Ditch Aqueduct on the Owasco Creek Outlet. The owner's yard was across the Outlet and the first sign said, "No Trespassing," which I ignored. As I walked along the trail I spotted a second sign about 20 feet ahead. As I neared the sign it read, "Don't you dare go any farther!" This caught my attention. I returned the way I came and knocked on the land owner's door. The lady of the house opened the door. The woman said, "I was wondering when you were going to ask permission!" I explained who I was, and what I would like to accomplish with my camera. She said it was all right to go ahead and take my photos. I happened to glance out the large bay window at the back of the room where she was standing. She was watching me all the time!

Postcard of four arch Port Byron aqueduct - author

Remaining single ditch aqueduct arch in Port Byron under the parking lot of St. John's Catholic Church - year 2000 - Liz Beebe in photo. The abutments measured six feet in thickness and the arch span was approximately 20 feet 4 inches with a height of 4 feet 9 inches (greatly filled in)

Sometimes I will wear my orange hard hat and spread maps on the hood of my truck. Many times people will leave their homes and come out to see what you are doing. It is then easy to explain your intentions and ask them for permission to enter their property, if you are still alive!

In Camillus, the adjoining Ditch Lock was located to the south of the Camillus aqueduct and the lock walls were contained within the aqueduct wing walls which gave the lock walls great support. The stone walls of the lock which measured 95 by 15 feet. The dirt fill backing the lock walls have eroded and slid into the lock proper forming a 45 degree angle of repose. The composite miter sill still remains on the north side of the lock.

The Ditch aqueduct sketch by Fenton Hanchett was drawn from new maps and measurements were taken in the bed of Nine Mile Creek. As described, the 120 foot aqueduct had two arches, with one abutment located in the mid-point of the creek. New information is continually being uncovered. The two main sources of information are from Craig Williams at the New York State Museum in Albany, NY and field work. There is no substitute for actual excavation and observation on site.

Side view of aqueduct and lock - Fenton Hanchett

The wide waters to the north of the aqueduct allowed boats to pull over to the berme and passengers to stay overnight at a rooming house on the present Thompson farm. The towpath ran on the west side of the aqueduct and then crosses over at the foot of the lock to the east side on a wooden bridge. With the towpath crossing from one side of the canal to the other, there were duplicate structures to provide services on both sides of the canal.

The Holmes Hutchinson maps of 1834, map no. 7-19, shows three buildings on the East side of the lock and three attached buildings on the West side. The latter buildings starting at the south were the stable, the grocery and the lock house. The L shaped building on the East was another grocery store. It had a basement with the foundation field stones still in place. The building measures approximately 27 feet on the north side and 30 feet on the west side. The foundation of loosely laid stone has been filled in with tree branches which must be removed for a more accurate measurement of the remaining foundation. A building to the south was another stable but this area has been regraded probably during the winter of 1844.

"The (Ditch) lock foundations are to consist of a solid flooring of hewed timber, one foot thick, and covered with well jointed three inch plank, over which, within the chamber, will be laid another flooring, of two inch planks, accurately fitted together with water joints , and spiked down, so as to prevent leakage; and this foundation is to be strongly supported and guarded by piling. The lock walls are to be not less than six feet thick, and to be sustained by several buttresses, to be laid in water-cement and thoroughly grouted." Canal Laws Vol. I - p. 412 - 1819.

"It is ascertained that a boat can be passed through a lock in five minutes; and that allowing for all contingencies, one can be passed every 8 minutes during 24 hours, making 180 each day." Canal Laws - Vol. II - p. 261.

They were also thinking of increasing the lock efficiency. "By doubling the locks, 360 (boats) can be passed daily. Two boats cannot pass each other upon any of the aqueducts; and the canals being but 40 feet wide on the surface, and 28 feet at the bottom and the boats 14 feet wide." It is always necessary to use one side of the Canal as a place of deposit, for articles to be transported and where boats may lie to load or unload."

"Boats must stop on one side or the other of the canal, to feed their horses or mules, to take in or discharge parts of their cargo, to repair their boats, to take on water. The boats must be out of the way of passing boats, and this could not be accomplished if a towing path were used on both sides of the canal." Canal Laws Vol. II - p. 261.

The source of water for the Jordan-Camillus summit level comes from several streams. A summit level is a raised level with locks at both ends lowering boats to a lower level.

1. Skaneateles Creek

2. Carpenters Brook

3. White-Bottom Brook

4. Nine Mile Creek Feeder - this feeder source is under discussion. We will attempt to prove the existence of this feeder in the chapter on feeders.

There was a remarkable collection of structures at the Camillus ditch lot site. The major structure was the 120 foot stone aqueduct which we have discussed in this chapter. The high side of Ditch Lock 58 uses the aqueduct walls to support the lock walls at the head of the lock. The towpath is on the south side of the Ditch prism. Towpaths in general, were placed away from the hillside (berme) as it was much easier to build-up the towpath from the soil removed than to cut the towpath into a hill.

The lock house lot of one acre was conveyed to the State of New York by Peter Brown, and the actual boundaries were surveyed by the State. We are in the process of resurveying the area.

The towpath also crosses from the south side to the north side approximately one mile to the west of Devoe Road. This site today shows a raised area in the ground running ninety degrees across the ditch prism which is the collapsed wooden change bridge.

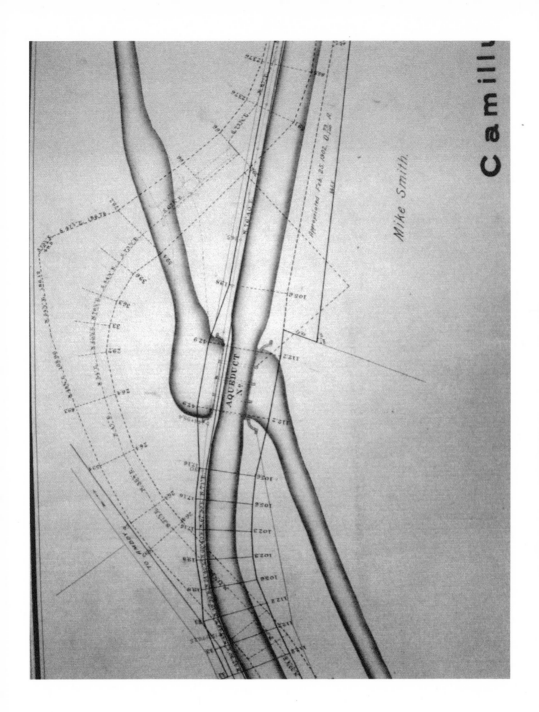

Schillner 1896
map

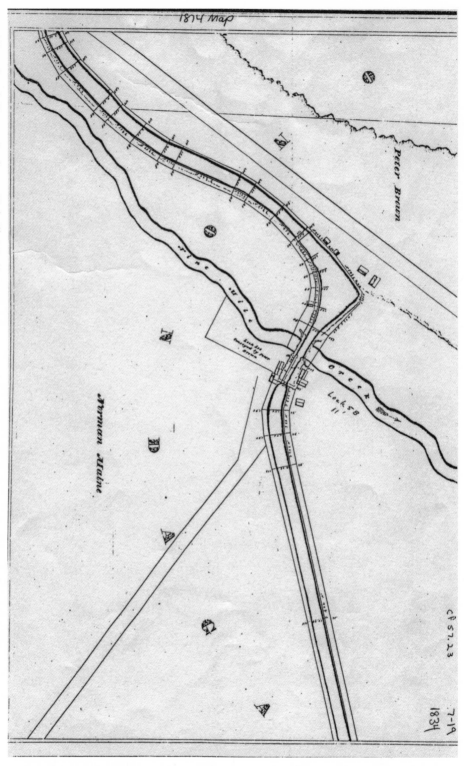

1874 Map

Peter Brown

Pine Will Creek

Lock for Damaged by Peter Brown

Lock 58
11'

cf 57.23

7-19

1834

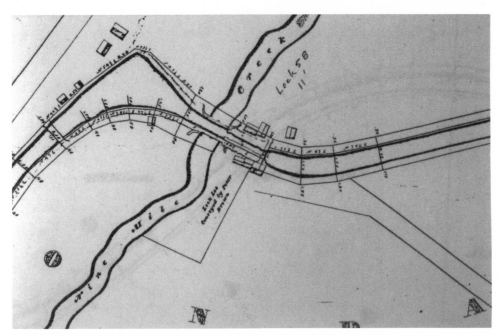

1834 - 7-19 - NYS Archives enlarged view

Rochester ditch aqueduct across Genesee River - CSNYS

The following description is taken from Assembly document No. 8 , annual report of the State Engineer and Surveyor, dated January 23, 1863. Water was let into the long level and navigated with great ceremony. The middle section completed was from Utica to the Seneca River 94 miles and the Salina side-cut 2 miles. The following is an extract from a book written in 1820 by Elkanah Watson describing the ceremony. "On the 22nd of October, 1819, the first boat sailed on the Erie Canal, from Rome to Utica. It was dragged by a single horse, trotting on the embankment, or towing-path. It was an elegant boat, constructed to carry passengers, and was called the "Chief Engineer," - a compliment to Benjamin Wright. The president and the Board of Commissioners, attended by many respectable gentlemen and ladies, embarked the ensuing day at Utica, with a band of music, to return to Rome. The scene was extremely interesting and highly grateful. The embarkation took place amid the ringing of bells, the roaring of cannon, and the loud acclamations of thousands of exhilarated spectators, male and female , who lined the banks of the new created river. The scene was truly sublime"

The "Chief Engineer" was built for passengers and was 61 feet in length and 7 1/2 feet in width with two "rising" cabins, of 14 feet each, with a flat deck between them.

Model of "Chief Engineer" taken by author at Rome Erie Village

The following is a brief summary of Clinton's Ditch and the First Enlargement in regard to canal facts.

It is expected that statistics be listed defining the original Clinton's Ditch and the First Enlargement. The following data is taken from the History of New York State Canals Volume two, p. 1030 by Noble E. Whitford, 1905.

The original canal was known as the Grand Canal and the popular name was Clinton's Ditch. See Ch. 4 on Dill's Landing. The construction began July 4, 1817 in Rome, New York and was completed Oct. 26, 1825 at an actual cost of $7,143,789.86. The length of the canal was 363 miles with a prism 40 feet wide at the top, 28 feet wide at the bottom and 4 feet deep.

There were 83 lift locks 90 feet long and 15 feet wide. Boats up to 75 tons used the canal.

The earlier canal was a tremendous success and a larger canal was badly needed. The First Enlargement was begun May 11, 1835 and the construction officially completed Sept. 1, 1862 at a cost of $36,495,535.00. The length of the canal was 350 1/2 miles long with a prism of 70 feet wide at the top, and 52 1/2 feet at the bottom and a depth of 7 feet. There were 72 lift locks with a length of 110 feet and a width of 18 feet. The boats increased in tonnage with a range of 210 to 240 tons.

The following photos depict the many problems encountered in digging the Erie Canal First Enlargement.

"Placing Struts in Marl Beds" March 1898 - note the small boards placed at an angle along the sides of the prism. Clay was used to line the bottom and sides of the canal. The boards, we believe, were placed as a guide for the laying of riprap stones to prevent the banks from washing out. OHA #11

"Placing Struts in Marl Beds" - March 1898 - timbers placed in ditches at bottom of canal for stabilization of soft bottom. Quicksand was present which is a bed of soft or loose sand saturated with water and having considerable depth. Note the piles in the foreground in an attempt to stabilize the bottom. OHA photo - second enlargement #10

PHOTO taken in marl beds showing the construction of a wooden towpath. The original towpath had disappeared due to the softness of the soil - OHA - #59

The Second Enlargement

The Erie Canal First Enlargement needed revitalization. Railroads were making a marked deleterious impact on the canal. They could carry more freight faster and cheaper year round. The canals eliminated tolls and lengthened locks to encourage more use. "The Nine Million Dollar" Improvement of 1895 was begun by the state. This called for deepening of the canal from 7 to 9 feet and raising the bridges thus enabling the canal to move cargo in larger boats. The Improvement of the 1895 was never completed throughout the state. The planning of the third enlargement, which was called the Barge Canal, was begun in 1905. It officially opened in 1917. The Barge Canal eliminated the need for towpaths and the use of mules . For the most part, the motorized boats used existing waterways and lakes.

In the Camillus area the Second Enlargement contracts from Lock 50 to west of Lock 51 in Jordan were let in 1896 and completed.

Chapter 3

THE CAMILLUS FEEDERS

A feeder is a channel, either man-made or natural that conveys water to the canal.

These feeders were controllable in order to maintain an adequate depth of water in the canal. The Nine Mile Creek, which flows through the Village of Camillus is a good example of a source which provides the water for a feeder.

Nine-Mile Creek originates at the outflow of Otisco Lake. The First Enlargement feeder was expanded in the 1870's. In 1869, $15,000 was spent on the Otisco Lake Reservoir providing the source of water for Nine Mile Creek and in 1872, the Otisco Lake Reservoir was completed. (p. 967 Whitford Vol.1) This glacial formed lake was damned at its northern end to provide an excellent source of water for the New York State Canal System.

We will discuss the formation of the 1834 millrace, and whether its waters were used to provide water to the Jordan level of the original canal commonly called Clinton's Ditch or the Grand Canal. Navigation was opened in the middle section of the Grand Canal in 1820 as stated in Vol. 1 of Whitford.

Millrace - Maxwell collection. Fishing on the Millrace banks in the Village of Camillus along the present Elm Street.

There was no direct mention of the Ditch feeder. In 1833, chapter 312 of Whitford, the Nine-Mile Creek feeder was to be made navigable. Since the Jordan level of the First Enlargement was not opened until the spring of 1846, the reference was probably made to the Ditch feeder. Noble E. Whitford was a resident engineer in the State of New York Engineer's Department and wrote a three volume History of the Canal System of the State of New York together with brief histories of the canals of the United States and Canada in 1906.

In 1841, Whitford states that the Nine-Mile Creek and Carpenter Brook feeders were finished. There is a mention made of an estimate for a feeder from Nine-Mile Creek, 3 miles long. For excavation of 42,242 cu. Yds. , dam, guard-gates, and grubbing there is a cost of $ 9,780.00. (p 158 - Pub. Doc. 1821.)

On May 18, 1831 The Nine-Mile Creek Association was formed to excavate and construct a two and one-half mile power canal, 20 feet wide . Waters for this millrace or raceway were diverted from Nine-Mile Creek at a site now covered by the New York Central Railroad embankment at Martisco. This raceway, according to Mary Maxwell, was also called the Nine-Mile Creek Canal. The millrace ended near Genesee Street in the Village of Camillus. Control gates allowed the excess water to leave the millrace and enter Nine-Mile Creek. This water later in 1846 entered the First Enlargement Nine-Mile Creek Feeder.

Millrace south of the Village of Camillus - Maxwell collection by permission.

One side of existing bridge over the millrace - 2002 by author

The millrace supplied water power for over nineteen mills. The following is a partial list of the mills that were along Nine Mile Creek. Starting in Marcellus, the Nightingale Feed Mill, Marcellus Feed Mill, Crown Mill, Marcellus Paper Company, Smith Barley Mill, Federal Mills, Camillus Wading Co., and Sims Mills. There were mills along the 1834 Millrace such as the Middlesex Knitting Mills, Harper Feed Mill, Roller Flour Mill, and a manufacture of pipe organ players. A steel bridge section still sits on its original site just below the end of the millrace which gave road access to several mills.

We have in our possession a copy of a DOT map showing the abandoned Erie Canal lands, sheet map number 621 dated 26 day June 1973. It lists the abandoned parcels by number and the easterly and westerly blue lines (outermost boundary-ownership lines) of the "1834 feeder" It shows the Ditch feeder entering the Grand Canal at the Dill area. This is the parcel along present day Newport Road which joins with listed Thompson Road and Camillus Road which is now Devoe Road. It also shows the First Enlargement Camillus Feeder joining with the Enlarged Erie Canal.

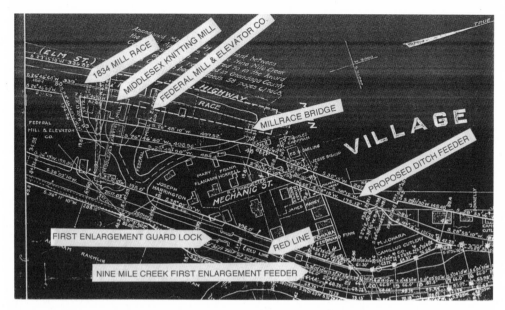

Map of mills and Nine-Mile Creek feeder.

An index map of abandoned lands of the Camillus Feeder with a scale of one inch equaling 500 feet lists the parcel numbers of the Ditch feeder. This feeder originated at a slightly lower level than the 1834 millrace. It lists the parcel numbers, map sheet number when abandoned, sold and purchaser.

Chronology of the Mill Race and Nine Mile Creek Feeder as listed in Whitford, Vol. One.

1. "In 1834 came the first step toward an enlarged canal. The Canal Commissioners submitted a special report (Assembly Documents, 1834, No 88) to the Legislature in relation to rebuilding the aqueduct at Rochester, taking an additional feeder into the Erie canal at Camillus on the Jordan level and doubling the locks upon the Erie canal east of the village of Syracuse." (p. 133 Whitford Vol. 1)

2. In 1833, Ch. 312, it is noted that the Nine Mile creek feeder was to be made navigable.

3. Fenton Hanchett translated a reference to the millrace in the Onondaga County Book of Deeds, Book 58, Pg. 61 "The Nine Mile Creek Canal Association claims damages on account of the State taking the Canal and the water thereof and the water of the Nine Mile Creek and the land covered by the canal, etc."

4. The claim of $7335.00 made by the Association from the appropriation of their land and water was paid.

5. In 1838, Ch. 269, p. 959 of Whitford, states that the Jordan level is to be cut down and the feeder is to be built at Nine Mile Creek.

It is interesting to note that since the Clinton's Ditch prism was eleven feet higher than the proposed First Enlargement, they were planning to cut the Jordan level down in 1838.

This probably means that they were not going to build a ditch feeder when the feeder for the first enlargement was already planned.

6. In 1841, the Nine Mile creek and Carpenter Brook feeders were finished. (p. 96 Whitford Vol.1) The following are the navigable feeders on the first enlargement.

Limestone creek feeder, Erie canal to Fayetteville 0.83 miles

Butternut creek feeder, Erie canal to feeder dam

above Dunlap's mills 1.67 miles

Camillus feeder, Erie canal to Camillus 1.04 miles

Delta feeder, foot of lock No. 9, Black River canal,

to Delta 1.40 miles

Black river feeder, Bonneville to head of pond

at Forestport 11.29 miles

(annual report of the State Engineer & Surveyor

1895, p. 237)

7. In 1845, the Jordan level was completed. (p. 960 Whitford Vol. 1)

The contracts for building the First Enlargement feeder (Nine Mile Creek Feeder) were let in 1838. The State dam was reported to be used for the first time in 1845. (C. Williams) The feeder dam is described farther in this chapter.

The physical evidence of a ditch feeder remains elusive. It would have cut through the heart of Camillus i.e.: Mechanics Street where there are houses today. The feeder would have run along the side of the hill along present Newport Road. Remember, that the elevation of Clinton' Ditch was eleven feet higher than the First Enlargement. Therefore, the feeder take-off from the millrace was obviously higher that the First Enlargement feeder. The elevation difference could support a ditch feeder.

Due to road construction, the higher elevation of the ditch feeder prism could easily be altered in the Village as well as along Newport Road. Along Camillus Road (Devoe) there had to be an embankment. This could easily have been used as fill for a wider road and to fill in the pond where the NYSDOT garage now stands. I do not remember any bank when I visited the crayfish pond as a teenager.

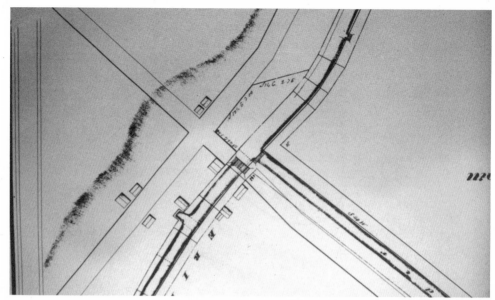

State map of 1922 showing portion of Erie Canal Lands. Shows 1834 ditch feeder connecting with Clinton's Ditch.

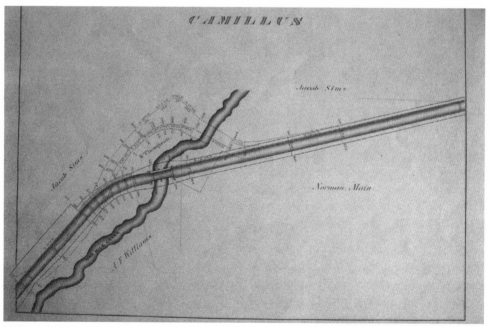

Holmes Hutchinson 1871 maps - The ditch feeder does not show on either the 1834 or the 1871 Holmes Hutchinson Maps

Example: 1247-1252 located in Village, with map sheet 258. It was abandoned August 15, 1929, sold December 7, 1929 to the Village of Camillus.

On December 24, 1997, I walked along Newport Road parallel to the first enlargement feeder. There is a depression to the west on the hillside where the State erected a chain-link fence. It is interesting to note that the New York State maps of State lands may hold the ditch feeder answer. The maps are dated the 20 day of December 1922. It is certified by Frank M. Williams, State Engineer and Surveyor and the Division Engineer, to be true and correct maps of the Camillus Feeder lands.

The Ditch Feeder was called the 1834 feeder. The feeder began at a lower level from the 1834 millrace, South of the Middlesex Knitting Mill. A portion of the millrace was abandoned May 1, 1835 by agreement between the Canal Appraisers and the Nine-Mile Canal Association - referred to in the award of that date and recorded in the Onondaga County Clerks office in book of deeds 58 pages 61 to 68.

The feeder red line is different than the first enlargement red line. Please refer to the chapter on Bench Marks. The abandonment maps show the feeder red line down the middle of the canal prism and not the inner angle of the towpath as located on the banks of the first enlargement.

The 1834 feeder paralleled the first enlargement feeder route, bending to the north-west at the Camillus Highway (Devoe Road).

The feeder connected with the 'Old Erie Canal'. A great amount of water was needed to supply water to Ditch Lock No. 58. The closest source of water was located to the west at White Bottom Brook. The 1834 feeder could provide the needed volume of water for the eleven foot lift at the lock.

Positive proof of the ditch feeder existence would be to obtain contract numbers and payments for work done as is available for the construction of the First Enlargement. These contract numbers have not been located to date.

The conclusion could be drawn that a ditch feeder was constructed around 1834, and was in use until the First Enlargement was in operation on the Jordan level in 1846. We have mentioned that the Nine-Mile Creek Feeder was completed in 1841, but was not put into use until 1846.

The following is in the report of the Canal Commissioners of 1833-34 No. 266, "In Assembly March 9, 1835." The act of May 6, 1834 "an act to improve the canals of this state" authorizes the Canal Commissioners to take the waters of the Nine-Mile creek in the Town of Camillus, for the supply of the Erie Canal, and construct such feeder as they shall deem proper, to conduct them to the Jordan level or summit:

- Nine Mile Creek Feeder. This feeder will extend from the road bridge near Samuel Dills, up the valley of Nine Mile creek three miles and fifty-eight chains, to the village of Camillus, (small letter - exact copy), a distance of one mile and five chains, it will be navigable. At this point it will cross the turnpike, and about thirteen chains Southerly, will rise about ten feet, and continue from thence in the canal of the Nine Mile Creek association to the creek near Perigo Austin's mills. By the appropriation the waterfall of the association will be reduced from about 23 feet to about 9 1/2 feet.

The feeder is deemed indispensable. If the Jordan summit of the Erie canal was cut down, it is believed the feeder would still be necessary. It might then be taken from the creek at a lower level. (end)

(p. 70) This feeder is to be introduced into the Erie Canal, to increase the supply of water on the Jordan level, in the town of Camillus. When completed, it will consist of the present Nine-Mile creek association's mill canal, of 2 1/2 miles in length, from Austin's to Camillus village, with such improvements as will be necessary to adapt it to use of the State, and a navigable feeder from the turnpike to the Erie Canal.

A waste-weir above the guard-gate, of 60 feet long, with stone abutments, to discharge freely, and regulate the water in floods. Located on the present Feeder Bank Road. First Enlargement

A feeder dam was constructed south of the Village of Camillus across Nine-Mile Creek. The feeder dam (no.8) spillway was 83 feet long and constructed of stone and wood. The three abutments were constructed of stone and can be viewed today.

"A new bulk head, the foundation and gates of wood, with abutments of masonry, well constructed and secured by two rows of sheet piling across the bottom each extending 6 feet into the embankment in the rear of each wall, and an embankment from the west side of the bulkhead to the hill, as indicated on the map"

Waste Weir. - author

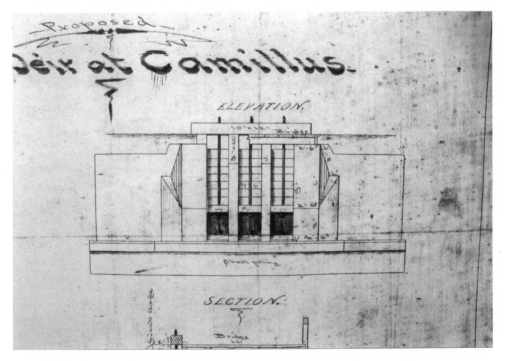

Plans of Camillus waste weir gates

Dam and entrance - Camillus feeder dam and bulkhead looking north. Nine Mile Creek is in foreground with spillway on right. OHA #17

Today - 2002 - author

The water from Nine-Mile Creek was shunted automatically into the feeder entrance due to the slope of the Creek bottom above the dam. If water was not needed in the feeder, or a smaller amount, one or all of the three control gates would be closed.

The Camillus feeder (no. 10) was 8,725 feet in length extending south of the First Enlargement.

There are two marvelous cut stone structures downstream from the feeder entrance. They may be the end boundary abutments to the navigable portion of the feeder. There are no slots in the sides in order to raise the water level with timbers. They were possible reminders that this was as far as the captain should take his boat.

The Nine-Mile Creek feeder was navigable from the First Enlargement through the Village of Camillus and ended at the grain mill and the Middlesex knitting mill.

The wide-waters allowed boats to enter directly under the grain mill for loading.

A guard gate was constructed downstream from the waste-weir. As was mentioned, in the case of a large amount of water coming down the feeder or the mill race, the guard gate beam gates could be closed thus stopping the water. The water would then leave the feeder by way of the waste-weir and into Nine-Mile Creek.

We asked the past mayor of Camillus, Morris Rachelin, if it would be possible for us to excavate the Village parking lot to view the walls of the guard lock. Morris laughed, and then I informed him that I was very serious about this proposal. He said no, but a strange incident occurred a few weeks later. The Village was excavating for the foundation of a small building and they uncovered the coping stones of the west wall along with the stone with the lock iron recesses. Morris asked me if we would like them in our canal park and today they are in position at the edge of the Sims' Museum parking lot.

Grain mill and knitting mill - author - 1981

It is interesting to note the following construction detail. "To excavate the stone and course material from the bottom and sides of the feeder where there are leaks, and replace the same at least one foot in thickness by good water-tight loam and clay, put in, to save all the water. This work shall be done with great care and faithfulness, as the water lost by filtration is entirely lost to the feeder. Some of the lining must be procured at a distance, but generally it can be obtained in the vicinity of the place it is wanted, by carting and wheeling."

The feeder went under the Camillus bridge, past the Camillus cutlery and past the German beer hall. There was a movable barrel bridge across the feeder to allow guests to visit the beer hall which basically was an island. The bridge would be swung back to allow boats to negotiate the feeder. Many of the drinkers would fall off the very insecure undulating bridge.

The feeder crossed a culvert of wood under the high embankment which was later replaced with a 42 inch cast iron culvert.

The feeder then enters the First Enlargement opposite the present site of the Sims' Museum.

The feeder towpath was on the west side of the feeder.

Placement of the lower end of pipe culvert under Camillus feeder. Note curved section of cutstone on ground in front of pipe. The workers are well dressed for manual labor. The culvert pipe was removed in the late 1970's. OHA # 8

POSTCARD - German
Beer Hall - Clarence
Curtis - note barrel bridge
used to cross feeder

First Enlargement
feeder taken from the
Route 5 bypass.

Chapter 4

DILL'S LANDING

Dill's home, which functioned as a hotel, was an important example of the many canal-side buildings that provided over-night accommodations for canal travelers.

The Dill's Landing site is located approximately 500 feet west of the present day Sims' Store Museum in Camillus. Unfortunately, a fire in 1945 destroyed most of the wooden structure of the building and today all that remains is the foundation.

An excellent definitive study of the Dill family lineage is presented in "Among the Hills of Camillus" by Mary Ellis Maxwell published in 1952. We will concentrate on the present Dill house remains which at this time is owned by Paul Dudden of Camillus.

Dill's Landing was an extremely important area on the Grand Canal (Clinton's Ditch) and also on the First Enlargement. The original canal was opened in this section in 1820. It was navigated through the 1844 season and was abandoned during the 1845 spring opening of the First Enlargement.

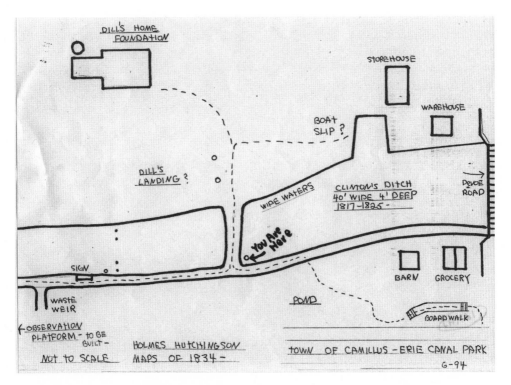

Field sketch of Devoe and Dill area. Beebe

"Samuel Dill was married in 1818 in Auburn, New York to Deborah Field and moved to an existing house about 1827 or 1828" (Hills of Camillus - Maxwell, Page 97)

"The kitchen part of the present farmhouse was then standing and the main part was built in 1829."

It is interesting to note that on the 12th day of November, 1834, Samuel Dill, on behalf of himself and John Dill, presented to the board of canal appraisers a claim of damages. This is recorded on Onondaga County Deeds, Book 90, p. 352.

Dill's house looking north-west - OHA (# 54)

Samuel Dill listed various complaints, but the major problem was the realignment of the canal (first enlargement) to the south of the present Clinton's Ditch and the digging of the Camillus feeder. Mr. Dill's business of storing and freighting will be transferred to the "village of nine mile creek" and their business will be injured to the amount of $1500. The citizens of the state have a right to change the places at which they will do their business. The appraisers stated that the change of the canal location does not constitute a claim for damages against the state. This item is, therefore, rejected. The state did pay the sum of $847 for the first five items in the claim. The claim was written by hand and as above, many of the words were not capitalized.

Dill's House looking north-east - OHA (#53)

Samuel Dill, once the canal route was changed sightly to the south, constructed a new store on the berme of the first enlargement. He constructed a wooden bridge from his home across the swampy area using hexagonal stones as bridge supports.

Photos show that there were three fireplaces in the house. The CSNYS (Canal Society of New York State) has a plain mantle piece in its collection along with two original shutters. The OHA in Syracuse has a second mantle collected by Richard Wright.

As a boy, I remember visiting the opened deserted house and saw legal papers scattered through out the entire two floors. These papers, which are extremely valuable, are slowly surfacing and being donated to us by individuals who visited the house. Donations include a cheese knife and a brass key from the front door.

Dill's house after fire - circa 1945 - photo obtained from Lorraine Pigula Dudden

The original canal presently widens from its usual 40 feet surface width and turns slightly north before crossing under the 1820 Camillus bridge (Devoe Road), to the east. There are no bridge remains from the ditch era. To the north in the wide waters (berme side) , there is a cut at nearly right angles to the canal. The approximate dimensions of the side cut are approximately 25-30 feet deep and approximately 25 feet across at entrance. Note that the sides taper from the parallel.

A possible use for this man-made cut, may have been to dock and unload a small boat. There is another possibility that it was used as a turning basin. It was too small to repair a canal line boat or a packet boat. There are no physical remains or maps to show that it was a dry dock. There was a warehouse and a storehouse on the north side and a barn and a grocery store on the tow-path side.

The canal prism in this area is in excellent condition. I remember as an early teenager, seeing a set of limestone stairs with 4 or 5 steps on the berme bank below the house foundation on the edge of the original canal. This would allow people that stayed in the Dill home to board their boat with ease. We have been unable to locate these stairs to date.

Drawing of the Dill area - Fenton Hanchett

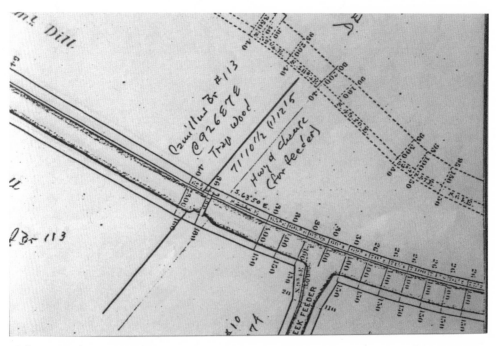

Holmes Hutchinson 1834 Map

Painting of Dill's Landing and the Nine Mile Creek feeder - by C. H. Curtis - displayed at Octagon House in 1970 - photo by author

There is a "waste - weir" located to the east which released excess water under the towpath into a pond to the south. This controlled the height of the water in this area. A second possibility for this structure is that it is a culvert. We plan to dig at a midpoint in the prism to possibly discover a stone-covered channel.

The area between the two canals, Clinton's Ditch and the First Enlargement were damned about 30 years age to create a wildlife habitat. This was done by the Federation of Sports Clubs with John Weeks of Baltimore Woods being the active member.

The highway bridge #113 was called the Camillus Bridge. It was a highway and a change bridge for the Nine-Mile Creek Feeder.

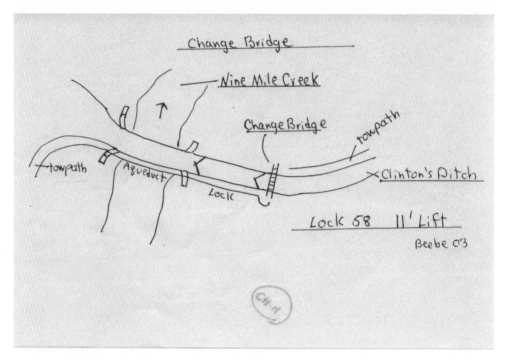

Sketch of our change bridge at the 1820 Clinton's Ditch lock-aqueduct site near present day Nine Mile Creek Aqueduct on the First Enlargement

The Camillus Bridge was made of wood and iron rods and was trapezoidal in form. The clear span was 71 feet, 10 1/2 inches in length and was 12 feet in width. There were no sidewalks for walkers. There was a second landing across from the present Sims' Store Museum. This is a vertical limestone wall extending approximately 300 feet. It is on the berme side of the canal to the east of the Camillus bridge.

Boats could off-load supplies for the nearby farms or for the villagers in Camillus. Boats that were entering the feeder from the west could wait here until the mules were brought over the bridge. The change bridge would allow the mules to cross the

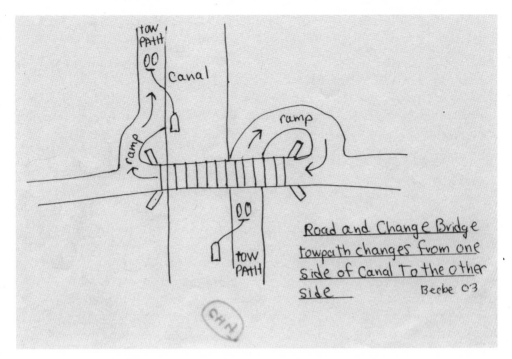

Sketch of change bridge to switch towpath to the opposite side of the canal.

bridge without unhitching. West bound boats heading into the feeder would coast into the feeder, unhitch the tow-line and wait for the mules to cross over the bridge. William Dzombak, in American Canals, November 1991, did an extensive study on force vector analysis in regard to mules pulling a heavily ladened canal boat and the forces exerted on the mules. We have noted that towpaths on the first enlargement are sloped away from the red-line, which is the edge of the towpath where it meets the slope or wall, toward the blue line ditch. This sloping provides a slope for water to drain off the towpath and avoids the creation of puddles. Mules do not like to walk through standing water. The above description applies to the Dill - Camillus area as well as the entire First Enlargement.

Dzombak writes that the towpath slopes away from the canal and this allows the mule to lean away from the canal and push against a sloped surface. The tendency when pulling a heavy load on a flat surface is to pull the mule toward the canal. The slope would neutralize this tendency. Constant maintenance had to be done on the towpath to keep it in optimum condition for the mules to pull the canal boats. In 1885 a "Champion Road Machine" or scraper was purchased by the Section Superintendent for eastern Montgomery County. The mule walking path created a depression that collected water. The machine removed the sod and gravel from the outside of the towpath and redistributed it in the low areas. Gravel was distributed on the towpath after the machine 'leveled' the area. Remember that there still will be a slope from the canal water to the drainage blue line ditch. (Sup. of Public Works - 1886-p. 21)

We have talked about the many problems involving the quicksand in digging the first enlargement in the Warners area. When we take new volunteers on field trips in these areas, we provide ten foot poles . We ask them to carry their poles horizontally in the event they start to sink. The pole will help them in being able to remove themselves from the soft sand and water. If we try to discourage a volunteer, we ask them to hold their pole vertically!

Occasionally, we are asked whether the water in the canal First Enlargement differs in height between locks. We remind the person asking the question that the water seeks its own level between locks and is always the same height. The only possible difference in height would be if a strong wind piles the water higher at one end for a short time. The height difference may seem to be different as many towpaths may no longer be level due to excavation, fill, wash-outs, etc. Water may be flowing between locks especially in long reaches, which may give the impression of a height difference. Breaches in either bank, streams now flowing into the prism, broken culverts, all would cause a current flow. Terracing, usually on the berme side may also be observed. This is the silt removed from the prism by dredging and piled and leveled. Occasionally, the spoils are deposited on the towpath side. High banks may be seen along the towpath or berme trails separating them from the blue line drainage ditches.

Chapter 5

NINE MILE CREEK AQUEDUCT
THE PAST, PRESENT, AND FUTURE

An aqueduct is a structure that carries a canal over a valley or a body of water. In Camillus the aqueduct spans Nine Mile Creek, hence its name.

The Nine Mile Creek aqueduct is the only First Enlargement aqueduct that can be restored and put into a navigable condition. Plans are underway to restore the aqueduct to its original specifications down to using wooden timbers as the base for the canal where it crosses Nine Mile Creek.

When re-building is completed, the aqueduct will become the star attraction of the Camillus Erie Canal Park and will be traversed by the museum's tourist boats.

This birds-eye view depicts a mule-drawn canal boat being pulled to the east over the Nine-Mile Creek Aqueduct in Camillus, New York. Of the 32 aqueducts constructed on the first enlargement, as listed in Vol. II of the History of New York Canals by Whitford (1905), only a few at the present time, are capable of carrying water.

Hanchett bird's-eye sketch #1

Nine Mile Creek Aqueduct – Circa 1870

Nine Mile Creek Aqueduct sketch of the reconstructed aqueduct circa 1870. Drawn and reproduced in our CSNYS publication "Bottoming Out". By Fenton Hanchett

Aqueduct looking north - author - 2002 #2

Drawing by Fenton Hanchett 1990 - photo by author

NINE MILE CREE
CONSTRUCTION -
CLINTON'S DITC
IN OPERATION.

Sketch of the Nine Mile Creek Aqueduct - Fenton Hanchett - 8-5-97

Two aqueducts have been restored to full width in concrete in the mid-1940's by the State of New York and at present carry water in their trunk. They are defined as non-navigable, but would be capable of boat travel. The first is located to the east of Canastota, New York, No. 3 over Cowassolon Creek and the second is No. 4 over Chittenango Creek on the middle division.

In Camillus, we have the Nine-Mile Creek Aqueduct built on the first enlargement between 1838 and 1841. It was not brought into service until the spring of 1845. The main sources of water such as Nine Mile Creek and Carpenter's Brook feeders were completed in 1841. The Jordan level was completed in 1845.

The existing structure was placed on the National Register of Historic Sites in 1976. According to the final estimate of the construction costs for the original structure , it contains 2976 cubic yards of masonry stone, 9414 feet of wood support piling, and 7795 cubic feet of hemlock support cribbing. The water carrying trunk used 11234 cubic feet of pine and oak support timber and 30293 board feet of pine and oak planking. (Hanchett)

The stone work is in excellent condition after an extensive five year restoration by our Erie Canal Volunteer Group. The group has removed tree roots, repositioned many limestone blocks and remortared the joints.

Pressure washing #3

Platform on pier showing mortaring #4 & #5

The Nine-Mile Creek Aqueduct is listed as No. 7 in the middle division located between locks No. 50 and No. 51. The total length of the four arch aqueduct is 144 feet and is considered the longest of the small aqueducts. There are four spans which have four gates and the interior width from berme to towpath is 49 feet.

We strongly felt that if we did not stabilize the remaining limestone piers in the aqueduct, it would only take a few years before the piers would be beyond the point of restoration. Due to the growth of tree roots and weeds, many of the limestone blocks were in danger of being pushed into Nine Mile Creek. We removed and slid the stones by hand, cut away the growth, and replaced the stones in their exact position on a mortar base. We hired a mason to work with us for over a year learning the various mortar mixes. He taught us formulas for horizontal mortaring as well as vertical mortar which tended to sag due to gravity. We made various tools to introduce the mix at least three inches into the space between the limestone blocks. We used for our course mix, 6 parts stone dust, 3 sand, 2 Portland Cement and 1 part type S cement. For our final mix for fine pointing we used 3 parts sand, 1 Portland cement and 1/4 to 1/2 parts type S cement. The pointing has held and the limestone blocks have remained sealed to this day.

Cement

In Whitford, Vol. 1, Benjamin Wright says: "The canal commissioners made no provision for the importation of cement. They appeared to think, that common quick lime would do for the work, although I suggested to them, in writing, in 1818, the propriety of making provision for cement, against the commencement of the year 1819, either by importing Tarras or Roman cement ... I have no hesitation in saying, that the discovery of hydraulic cement by Mr. White, had been of incalculable benefit to the State, and that it is a discovery which ought, in justice, to be handsomely remunerated." (Assembly Journal, 1824, pp. 1007-1008) The structures built with common lime mortar soon failed.

Water proof lime was first discovered by Canvass White in 1818 and patented by him in 1820. "The Canal Commissioners stated in their report for 1820, that they had discovered water-proof lime in the progress of their exertions, in the quarries of Madison, Onondaga, Cayuga, Ontario, and Genesee counties: that it must be pulverized and mixed one-half sand to one of lime". (Annual Report of the State Engineer and Surveyor-1863, p.114) There is an extremely complete and excellent booklet on "The Erie Canal and Cement" by Robert F. Nostrant. (2001)

The contract for constructing the Aqueduct over Nine-Mile Creek was signed October 4th, 1838. This was an agreement between Samuel M. S. Denton and Andrew E. Cromwell and the Canal Commissioners of the State of New York. "The contractors agree that they will furnish all the materials, which shall be of a sound and good quality, and perform all the labor necessary to construct and finish in every respect in the most substantial and workmanlike manner, an Aqueduct over Nine Mile Creek in Section No. II of the Jordan level."

Denton and Cromwell twice petitioned the State's Canal Board for extra monies for the construction of the aqueduct. In 1842, there were extra costs incurred from the failure of the State to lower the water. The builders understood that the State would, on a temporary basis, remove the dam impounding the water. This was done at the beginning as the foundation for the abutments and piers were being built. The mills downstream soon convinced the State engineers that it would be cheaper to pay the contractors damages than to pay the mill owners what they demanded due to loss of water power. Denton and Cromwell were forced to erect an expensive 610 foot coffer dam. The coffer dam had to be inspected constantly and water had to be pumped out of the actual aqueduct construction site. The coffer dam broke six times and the contractors asked for $5,000 in compensation and received one-half that amount. (NYS Archives, Canal Board Papers, Series A1140, 1842, Package 22) (C. Williams field guide 1999)

The second petition came a year later. They claimed that in the spring of 1840 they were directed "by the engineer having charge of the work to use mortar composed of one half cement and one half sand whereas previous to that time it had been customary

68

to use it in the proportion of one part cement to two of sand." They were awarded the full claim by the Canal Board. NYS Archives, Canal Board Papers, Series A1140, 1843, Package 6)

The last payment to the contractors for the completion of the Aqueduct was made on June 3 , 1842 with a total cost of $51,668.43. (Annual Report of the Canal Commissioner 1839 p.16) There is a very interesting clause at the end of the contract. "And the said Contractor further promise and agree that they will not of themselves or by there agent or agents, give or sell any ardent spirits to these workmen, or any other person" There are many stories allowing whiskey to be consumed as a reward for performance especially in the digging of the canal prism.

Removing brush growth - June 1992 - author

Spillway on south-west portion of Nine Mile Creek aqueduct to allow an escape for excess water - OHA # 57

I did not realize at the onset of this restoration that many of the men did not appreciate snakes. I would show the snakes to them out of interest. Many said later that they were not fond of snakes, but did not want to hurt my feelings. On the work days, I would go onto the aqueduct and hand pick the snakes and take them into the nearby woods. When the next work session arrived, the same snakes were back on the aqueduct sunny themselves, and I would remove them again.

While working on the aqueduct, some members have fallen off boats, tipped over canoes, and slid into Nine Mile Creek. We would work in all conditions. Sometimes we would lose things out of our pockets while climbing onto ladders. At times the scaffolding would slip from the pier, and we would end up in Nine Mile Creek. We always carried extra clothes. In Sims' Museum we have a plaque honoring the Underwater Demolition Team that commemorates the many volunteers that have accidentally fallen into the canal or Nine Mile Creek.

Wood was plentiful in the region. The contract specifies that the oak and pine timber shall be cut in the month of February after the date of the annexed contract. It further states that the timber shall be sawed or hewed as the case may be, by the first day of June following, and set up under proper cover in such a manner as to most effectually promote its seasoning.

Spacer "Stones" - East end of aqueduct -
shows rotted timbers- author

The wooden elements in the aqueduct needed constant maintenance and replacements. Wooden trunks would last on an average of 8 to 10 years. Many of the timbers were placed tightly together causing the retention of moisture and ultimate dry rot. The contractors did use spacer stones (ours were concrete) at the ends of the aqueduct to space the support timbers resting on the piers to promote air circulation.

By the mid-1850's, the aqueduct was reported to be "very much decayed and has required much care". A new timber trunk came in 1857. The new trunk for the Nine Mile Creek Aqueduct cost $4,408.57. The next and last reported retimbering of the trunk came in 1895. (Annual Report of the Canal Commissioners, 1857, p.76-77 - 1858, p. 58 - 1876, p. 79 - Annual Report of Supt. of Public Works, 1896, p.150)

In 1868 a heavily laden boat "came into contact" with and carried away a portion of the aqueduct. (Annual Report of the Canal Commissioners, 1869, p. 44) We knew for years that about 60 feet of the towpath and berme had been altered to the east of the aqueduct, but we did not have the following description until Craig Williams located it in the State Archives. The towpath twist wall and the berme slope walls were missing. The only structures on site were various lengths of concrete which had been used to shore up the banks. The towpath level drops about two feet to the east from the towpath height. A sloping, cut limestone block shows the slope in the towpath level.

Towpath grade difference - author
The towpath to the east of the aqueduct is at a lower towpath level.

THE BREAK OF 1882: The following excerpts are taken from the Annual Report of the State Engineer and Surveyor 1883, p. 78-79, and the Annual Report of the Superintendent of Public Works 1883, p. 56.

"A break occurred early Friday morning, September 15, through the berme bank of the Erie Canal, at the east end of Nine Mile Creek Aqueduct on the Jordan level, suspending navigation until three PM Sunday, September 24 - and interval of nine and a half days. And although but about sixty feet in length of the bank was carried away, still it was a serious break, and a difficult one to repair, for the reason of its location (right at the end of the aqueduct), and from the fact that TWO BOATS caught in the break had to be disposed of. The boats caught and hung by one end each upon the east end of the aqueduct trunk floor, and the twelve miles of water from the level, west of the break, pouring through the aqueduct, scoured out the earth from underneath them to a depth of twenty-two feet below canal bottom. This caused about sixty feet in length of the towing-path bank, for half its width, to slide into the canal, carrying with it its vertical and slope walls, Serious apprehensions were felt for the safety of the aqueduct, for it hardly seemed possible that the earth could be swept away close to the structure to so great a depth without undermining and causing its failure. But upon constructing a coffer dam and pumping out the water sufficiently low to admit an examination, the aqueduct was found to be unharmed. Great credit is due those in charge of the structure, when built, for the substantial manner in which the work was done; otherwise it surely would have failed under so trying an ordeal, and its failure at this time would have suspended navigation upon the Erie Canal for the balance of the season. In repairing the break, the material at hand for embankment and puddling was not of the best, therefore great care was necessary in its selection and manipulation to make the work secure. The boats were cut to pieces and removed, except such portions of them as were entirely below canal bottom and at least twenty feet away from the aqueduct. The decks were removed from these and earth filled in, around and over them to canal bottom. It required about 6,000 cubic yards of material to replace the banks and the prism below canal bottom carried away by the break."

It is confidently believed that the break was caused by muskrats. The discoveries made when replacing the break, and the numerous leaks they have caused in that vicinity since then, justifies such a conclusion. Old canal men say they never knew them to be so troublesome before. It has been only by constant watching, timely discoveries and prompt action, that several leaks they have recently caused did not result in serious breaks.

The aqueduct received extensive repointing with the 1895 Improvement. The last documented repairs to the aqueduct came in 1916 when "braces have been placed ... to strengthen the cap timber on the berme side." (Annual Report of the Superintendent of public Works 1917, p.177)

Looking south showing buggy on aqueduct - OHA #18

Boats on aqueduct - OHA - negative not sharp - note coping stones on left with a 2 inch overhang. - #52

The following are excerpts from various Canal Commissioner reports describing the aqueduct.

a. Section No. 9 - 1851-55- p. 55 - "Section begins at Lock No. 50, three miles west of Syracuse, and extends west thirty-four miles to the east line of Wayne County".

b. 1857 - p 76-77 - "Nine Mile Creek aqueduct is very much decayed and has required much care to sustain it in navigable condition during the season. The repairs upon it have amounted to $389.50. The Nine Mile Creek aqueduct will require rebuilding this spring, for which the timber has been obtained at a cost of about $2,800. The Jordan aqueduct and Nine Mile Creek Aqueduct were constructed in 1840 and have lasted till now without serious repairs".

Story - Discovery of coping stones. The entire row of cap or coping stones are missing from the wall along the tow-path side of the aqueduct. These stones acted as a protective rain cap to protect the underlying wall. They extended over the edges two inches and the seams between the stones were fully sealed with mortar. I talked with a Dan Mordell, a long time canal expert, on one of our Canal Society field trips. I asked Dan if he knew who removed the entire length of coping stones along the tow-path. He said they were pushed (i.e.; front-end loader) into Nine-Mile Creek. I slipped into my wetsuit and entered the water on the north side of the aqueduct. I waded through waist-deep water and tripped over the first coping stone. To date, we have raised, with difficulty, ten straight and one curved coping stones. I estimate that between 30 and

35 stones were on the aqueduct as the exact plans of construction have not surfaced in the archives in Albany. The mud is 10 feet deep and the suction to raise the remaining stones is tremendous. Removal of the mud using high pressure water hoses has been tried on a small scale with limited success.

Coping stones (Post card - Todd Weseloh)

Raising coping stone from north side of aqueduct - author.

The original creek bed passed to the east of the enlarged Nine-Mile Creek Aqueduct. Fenton Hanchett estimated that 8,227.00 cu. yds. of earth were excavated forming the foundation pit where the aqueduct was constructed. This excavated earth was mounded to the east forming a berme separating the Nine-Mile Creek from the excavation pit. This enabled the workers to form the bottom of the pit as well as to drive piles, build the foundation of timbers and lay stonework in relatively dry conditions. Wood and stone could be delivered to the site by canal boats using the Clinton's Ditch. Clinton's Ditch was located approximately 100 yards to the north.

Hanchett sketch showing diversion of creek. Ditch Aqueduct 1820 at top and construction of Nine Mile Creek Aqueduct at bottom.

Excellent limestone, the finest in the state, could be obtained at the Split Rock Quarry. Originally stone was cut and paid for at the quarry. The stone was delivered by carts to the aqueduct site, but quite often a few mysteriously disappeared in route. The State then decided to pay for the stone upon delivery and suddenly very few stones disappeared on their way to the building site.

The Canal Commissioners report continues and states, "The stone in the masonry shall be well beded in hydraulic cement made of the best hydraulic lime and clean sharp sand in such proportions as the said Engineer may direct"

Our stone piers are thirty-one feet apart which is a large distance for wooden timbers to span. It is unfortunate that the original designers and builders did not add another pier as this would make a more workable span distance. Lumber was cheaper and more readily available than limestone. Originally the trunk was caulked by boat builders using oakum and tar. The main trunk support timbers measure 9" by 16" and are 36 feet long. (pier to pier) The wood used was pine. A second massive timber called a straining piece was placed under this main timber for additional support. This measured 9" by 9" and was 16 feet long and was of oak. Oak braces measuring 9" by 9" and 9 feet long supported the straining piece. Notches were placed in the piers to receive these braces a approximately a 45 degree angle.

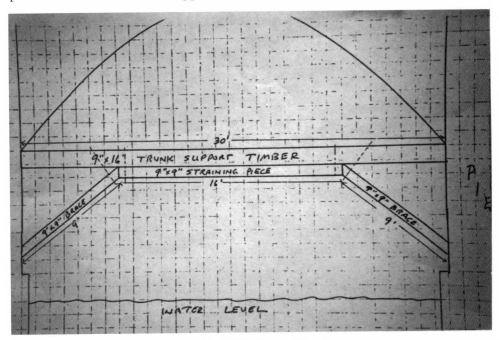

SKETCH OF FOUNDATION OF TRUNK. Fenton Hanchett

I was in Nine Mile Creek with my wet suit attempting to locate any bench marks or mason marks on the aqueduct. Most of the canal structures do not have any of these marks or builder identification descriptions. I have described in another chapter the marks or plaques that have been located. Marshall Bishop, one of our volunteers, was on the NE corner wing wall of the Nine Mile Creek Aqueduct, and he yelled down to me in the water. "I see a pin or nail under my foot which may be important!" Marsh had discovered the copper plug located on the NW corner of the coping of the east retaining wall, towpath side as placed in the 1901 survey of canal structures.

Aqueduct scuba dive - The date was October 6, 1990 and I dove into Nine Mile Creek under the aqueduct to ascertain the condition of the hemlock flooring that was placed along with wooden skirts, to protect and prevent scouring of the aqueduct due to the creek current. The duration of the dive was one hour to a maximum depth of nine feet. My wife, Liz, was the safety person standing on the pier with a line attached to me. I used a single tank of air. Gloves were worn due to the large collection of glass on the floor.

Actual wood trunk foundation. These photos show decaying aqueduct floor on the east side and the flooring remaining on the south side - Jane Maxwell - by permission from Jane Maxwell

I measured the distance from the top of the lower support pier to the top of the hemlock floor. It was exactly 12 feet. The hemlock flooring is in excellent condition. Due to its hardness and being well preserved under water, I was unable to stick the blade of my scuba knife into the wood . Wood will remain in a preserved state as long as it remains underwater. When timbers are exposed to the air and oxygen in a wet condition, they will deteriorate rapidly.

Out of curiosity, the water snakes would approach me on the surface . I splashed them, and they moved away. Underwater I attracted a few leaches which loosely attached themselves to my face mask. The 90 degree angle between the wooden floor and the stone pier is sealed. Excess caulking or tar can be felt oozing out between the floor joints.

The more expensive aspect of this restoration is the reconstruction of the wooden trunk. The trunk represents approximately twenty per cent of the completed structure (Fenton Hanchett). Our main goal is to restore this trunk so a boat can travel from Sims' Store Museum over the aqueduct eastward to route 173, a total distance of over two miles. This will be the only restored navigable aqueduct on the first enlargement in the State of New York.

In the future I plan to write a book detailing exactly how the Nine Mile Creek Aqueduct was restored. The aqueduct structure will be reconstructed using modern materials to resemble the historic original. The stringers will be fabricated of southern yellow pine and glue laminated for strength and stability. The timber floor, walls, and other elements also will be from glue laminated timbers. The entire structure will be treated with a wood preservative to discourage rot and decay. Attachments and connections will be accomplished using modern timber construction hardware.

These devices will be disguised by placing them in countersunk holes and plugging them with dowels. The planking will be joined with a tongue and groove joint that will allow the boards to expand and contract with fluctuations in moisture content. To reinforce the water-tightness of this joint, gasket material will be placed in the groove in such a way that the boards will swell into contact with the gasket, forming a tight seal. (Clough, Harbour & Associates - draft - May 2000)

We have been informed that the glulam construction is guaranteed for fifty years. The estimated cost of restoring the project before going to bid is $2,225,000.00.

There are two aqueducts of importance that have been restored. The first aqueduct is the Tohickon Creek Aqueduct at Point Pleasant, Pennsylvania on the Delaware Canal. The second aqueduct was restored by the National Parks Service, and it is the Delaware (Roebling) Aqueduct which carried the Delaware and Hudson Canal over the Delaware River. The D & H Canal carried coal from Honesdale, Pennsylvania to Kingston, New York on the Hudson River.

Nine Mile Creek aqueduct showing original timbers - Circa: 1940 OHA #63

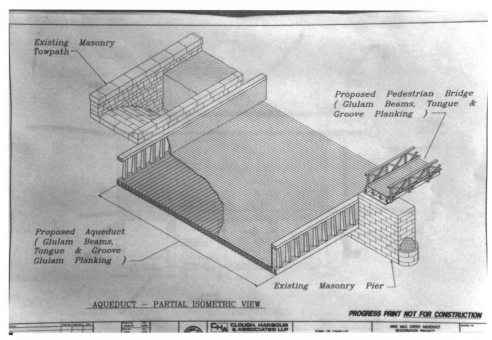

Drawing of aqueduct partial isometric view - Clough, Harbour and Associates, LLP

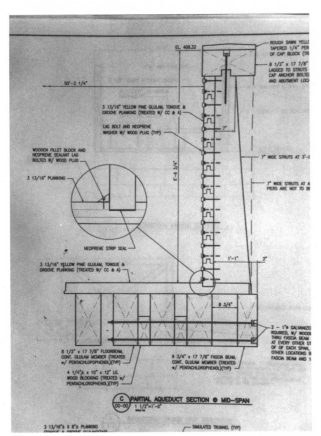

EL. 408.32

50'-3 1/4"

ROUGH SAWN YELLO
TAPERED 1/4" PER
OF CAP BLOCK (TR

8 1/2" x 17 7/8"
LAGGED TO STRUTS
CAP ANCHOR BOLTE
AND ABUTMENT LOC

3 13/16" YELLOW PINE GLULAM, TONGUE &
GROOVE PLANKING (TREATED W/ CC & A)

LAG BOLT AND NEOPRENE
WASHER W/ WOOD PLUG (TYP)

7"

7" WIDE STRUTS AT 3'-6

7" WIDE STRUTS AT A
PIERS ARE NOT TO BE

WOODEN FILLET BLOCK AND
NEOPRENE SEALANT LAG
BOLTED W/ WOOD PLUG

3 13/16" PLANKING

NEOPRENE STRIP SEAL

3 13/16" YELLOW PINE GLULAM, TONGUE &
GROOVE PLANKING (TREATED W/ CC & A)

1'-1"

2"

8 3/4"

6'-8 3/4"

8 1/2" x 17 7/8" FLOORBEAM,
CONT. GLULAM MEMBER (TREATED
W/ PENTACHLOROPHENOL)(TYP)

4 1/4"± x 10" x 12" LG.
WOOD BLOCKING (TREATED W/
PENTACHLOROPHENOL)(TYP)

6 3/4" x 17 7/8" FASCIA BEAM,
CONT. GLULAM MEMBER (TREATED
W/ PENTACHLOROPHENOL)(TYP)

2 – 1"ø GALVANIZED
REQUIRED, W/ WOODE
THRU FASCIA BEAM
AT EVERY OTHER ST
OF OF EACH SPAN,
OTHER LOCATIONS B
FASCIA BEAM AND 1

C
00-00 PARTIAL AQUEDUCT SECTION @ MID-SPAN
1 1/2"=1'-0"

3 13/16"± X 8"± PLANKING

SIMULATED TRUNNEL (TYP)

A cross section of Glulam construction - drawings from Clough, Harbour and Associates LLP

Tohickon Creek aqueduct on Delaware Canal - author - 2001

Delaware aqueduct at Lackawaxen, Pine County, Pennsylvania (near side) and Minisink Ford, Sullivan County, New York (far side) - author - 2001

Chapter 6

Locks

A lock is an enclosed chamber, with gates at each end, for raising or lowering vessels from one level to another by admitting or releasing water.

There were three types of locks in use on the Erie Canal First Enlargement: miter gate lift locks, guard locks, and weighlocks.

Due to the various changes in elevation of the New York State landscape, 72 lift locks were required on the First Enlargement to allow the canal boats to travel from Albany to Buffalo, a distance of 350 1/2 miles.

The very first lift lock constructed for the First Enlargement is located at Gere's Lock in the Town of Camillus.

I asked Richard Wright, who was the founder of our Canal Society of New York State, to correct a canal paper that I was writing. There were many corrections which he marked in the left margin. At the bottom of the page and again in the left margin, he placed two words in quotation marks, and they read, "Had enough?"

Gere's Lock , No. 50, is located at the eastern extremity of the Town of Camillus. The Geddes culvert (Geddes Brook), with two stone arch openings, is immediately to the east of the lock, extending 124 feet in length under the First Enlargement. Both of the openings have a span of 4 feet and a height of 3 feet.

We will discuss Gere Lock as a typical prototype of the first enlargement locks, but we will emphasize several major differences.

The boats that would enter Gere's Lock No. 50 in Camillus were built to standard plans. The Canal Commissioner Report of 1856, p. 160, states "Boats were built 97 1/2 feet long and 17 feet 8 inches wide. The draft shall not exceed 6 feet below the surface of the water. The height above the water is also restricted and shall not exceed 11 feet 1/4 inches above the surface of the water. The heavier built boats on the Erie Canal weigh 75 tons and the boat and cargo of the largest class weigh 290 tons. Boats built of pine sides run about 6 years without extensive repairs."

Boat Sizes

Batteaux - 18 to 24 feet long.

Durham Boats - 60 feet long.

Original Erie Canal or Clinton's Ditch - 78 feet long, 14 1/2 wide.

First Enlargement - 97 1/2 feet long, 17 1/2 wide.

The photo above shows the steam powered packet boat, the Walter McMullin, in the lengthen berme chamber in Lock No. 50. The Walter McMullin was built in the Baldwinsville boat yard by the Brown Boat Company and the steam engine was built by the Morris Machine Works. The boat ran from Jordan to Syracuse and back every day except Sunday. The McMullin arrived at Clinton's Square in Syracuse at 10:00 A.M. and returned to Jordan at 3:00 P.M. It cost 5 cents one way. - OHA circa 1895

Note the lock shanty between the lock chambers and Coakley's store on the right. The boat "Kate" preceded the Walter McMullin. The photo was taken from the end of the berme chamber looking west. Gere's bridge is in the background and the salt sheds are seen to the right of the barn. Michael Coakley opened a store at Gere's Lock and operated the store until 1886. Frank Pettrone bought the store from Michael Coakley for the sum of $2,800.00.

A painting of Gere's Lock owned by Frank A. Pettrone, M.D. (photo sent by Dr. Pettrone)

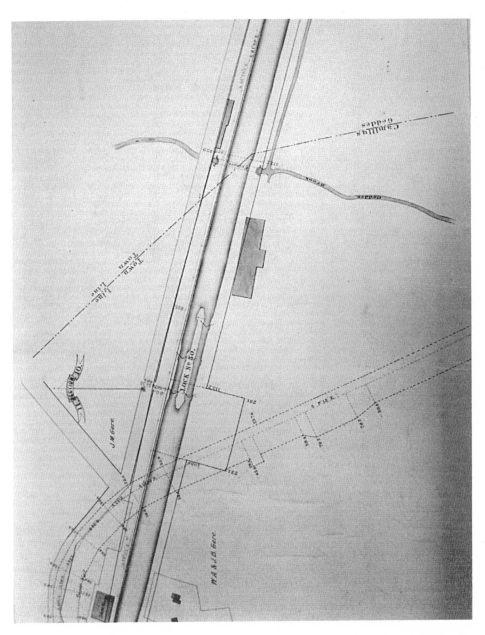

Schillner 1896 Map of Gere Lock No. 50 - shows Geddes culvert flowing north under first enlargement. Note: Clinton's Ditch in dotted lines on left side.

C. M. Warner - Looking north-east from Gere Bridge - OHA. Note on the boat the sewer pipe, baskets, barrels, and watermelons. Gere's salt warehouse is on left and the salt vats are behind. The NYS Fair buildings are in the distance and Mike Coakley's barn and house are on the right side across the canal.

Passing

In general, boat operators followed the rule of "right". The boat pulled by mules heading west would keep his boat along the towpath bank. The oncoming boat heading east would have to accomplish two maneuvers. The hoggie would turn the mule team 90 degrees to the left facing away from the canal and come to a complete halt. The captain would steer the boat toward the berme and since the boat still had momentum, the towline would drop to the bottom of the canal. Towlines were made of hemp and were 150 to 200 feet long. The west bound mules would walk over the towline and the boat being pulled would pass over the towline resting on the bottom of the canal.

Gere's Lock was a lift-lock to the west with the lift from the lower miter-sill of 7.965 feet. The size of the double lock chambers are 110 feet long by 18 feet wide. In 1884, Lock no. 50 was lengthened to pass 'double headers' with this being the first lock extension to be undertaken. (Whitford Vol 1, p. 969) This lock lengthening to 220 feet was completed in 1885.

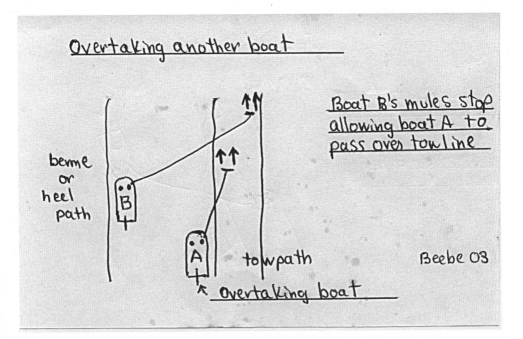

Overtaking another boat

berme
or
heel
path

B

A

N

towpath

↑ overtaking boat

Boat B's mules stop
allowing boat A to
pass over towline

Beebe 03

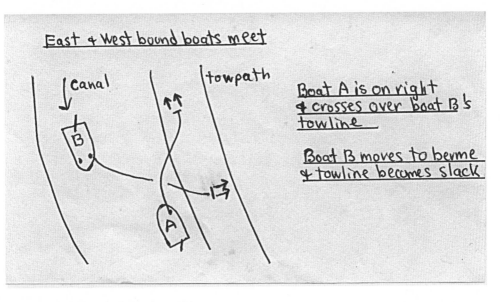

East & West bound boats meet

Canal

towpath

B

A

13

Boat A is on right
& crosses over boat B's
towline

Boat B moves to berme
& towline becomes slack

Drawings a) East and west bound boats meet
          b) overtaking another boat

87

Berme chamber as it looks today, looking northwest - by author

Berme extension and towpath approach - looking SW - author (photo B)

Two photos placed together showing entire lock - looking SW - photo taken by Charles H. Billings on November 5, 1948 - OHA #60

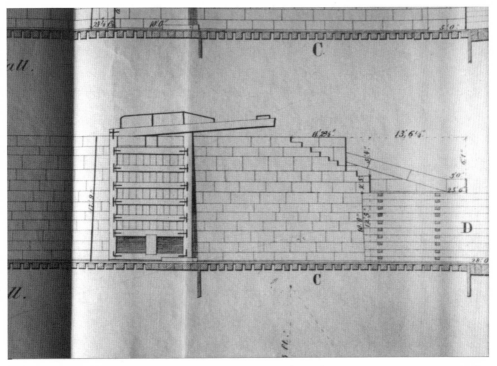

Lock foundation - wooden pier (D) - foundation (C) shows lower gate

Gere's enlarged Lock No. 50 - CIRCA 1897-98 - looking to west at newly constructed berme chamber extension - note overflow exit opening and Coakley's store on right. "Nine Million Dollar Improvement" (#4) OHA

Gere's Lock south chamber - note wooden floor timbers, cross-over bridge, wooden pier on right and the absence of lock gates. OHA # 5

Gere's Lock looking east - note lock shanty and Solvay Process plant in background. Slightly out of focus. OHA #6

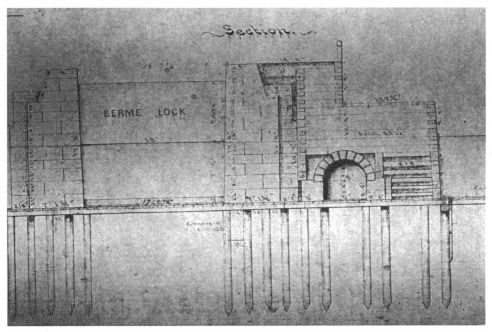

Wood foundation pilings - exit tunnel extended entire length of the lock - extended berme lock chamber - State Archives - (F)

All of the lock stones used in the construction of this lock rest on oak and hemlock timbers supported by hundreds of wooden pilings 16 feet long. Concrete was used between the foundation timbers.

The double lock allowed lockage in both directions thus shortening the locking time. In 1867, tests were made on Lock no. 30 (10.5 foot lift) to determine the time needed for lockage. In the trial 194 boats were locked. The minimum time was three minutes and the maximum time was eleven and one-half minutes with the average being five minutes and 12 seconds. (p.273 - Whitford II) With double locks, 562 boats could be locked through in 24 hours. The two Syracuse towpath chambers in lock No. 47 and 48 were widened two feet. The berme chambers were also widened in 1874. This widening allowed for easier movement of water past the boats and thus shortened the locking time.

The canal builders were extremely fortunate in having an excellent source of quality limestone in the area. The main source of stone for Gere Lock was at the Split Rock Quarry. Smaller quarries were located along Route 173 and at a site along Munro Road in Camillus.

All seventy-two lift locks were doubled eventually with the exception of weigh-locks (not a lift lock), side cuts and guard locks. (see Whitford Vol. II)

On a Canal Society of New York State field trip, we were investigating a very well preserved lock no. 29 at Fort Hunter. I noticed that five or six people were leaning over the edge of the lock into the lock chamber. I approached the group and commented how environmentally sound it was for them to clean the weeds between the limestone blocks. This would prevent further deterioration of the mortar remaining between the stones. They cheerfully replied that they were planting wildflower seeds so the lock walls would be a myriad of color when the seeds germinated. Perception is not everything.

Wooden piers were constructed at the middle of the locks between the lock chambers at the high and low ends of the lock. This provided a step-off platform for the boatman to gain access to the lock. The pier timbers are separated horizontally near the top so that water can flow between them into the overflow portals. Debris can also be strained. The pier covers the portal entrances preventing anyone from accidentally falling into the pit.

Block and tackle were used prior to the introduction of the turbine, to move boats in and out of the locks.

Gere's Lock looking southeast - towpath lock chamber -note lock shanty, lantern, turbine mechanism, and the man in the white shirt is resting on the balance beam. c. 1900 (#62) OHA

The three entrance portals at the head of the lock, at an average, measure 46 inches wide and 40 1/2 inches in height. There are grooves cut at the sides of the three portal entrances. Boards could be placed in these slots to increase the water height on the high side of the lock. This would give a greater head of water to turn the turbine.

In 1882 , turbines, devised by Dennison Richmond , were used in the lock pit "for hauling boats, prove of great utility." (Whitford, p.969) The surplus water or hopefully an adequate normal water flow, turned the horizontally placed turbine at the head of the lock.

The plan for the turbine is titled "General Machinery Plan for Drawing Boats into Locks", dated July 2, 1889. The turbine mechanism aided in quicker lockages. When these turbines were installed, at Lock No. 54 (1888), boats were passed (locked through) in 9 minutes and 40 seconds and at Lock No. 56, in 10 minutes (Whitford, p. 334) "A turbine wheel, set in the wall at the head of the lock, and discharging through the culvert under the central pier wall, operated rope cables which, passing over spools, were used to haul the boats into and out of the lock." This sentence, which is a bit awkward, expresses the turbine best. Wire cables were tried, but proved to be heavy to overhaul and wore and broke easily. (Whitford, p. 334)

Decayed wooden pier and the three water entrance portals - note the lock gates are in place with a debris fence catcher in front. Allied Chemical is in the background. Also note that the lock shanty roof is aligned north and south which is different from the photo of the Walter McMullin. Looking North East c. 1920 OHA (#1)

The Introduction of Turbines

The gate shaft is fastened to the rear wall of the pit by stands. The shaft ends in a 22 inch diameter wheel with buckets 10 inches deep. This is designed for a lift of seven feet. The main miter wheel could turn the horizontal shaft at a speed of 56 rpm with adequate water supply. A Frisbie's friction clutch was used at both ends of the horizontal 2 7/8 inch thick shaft to control the speed of the spool holding the rope cables.

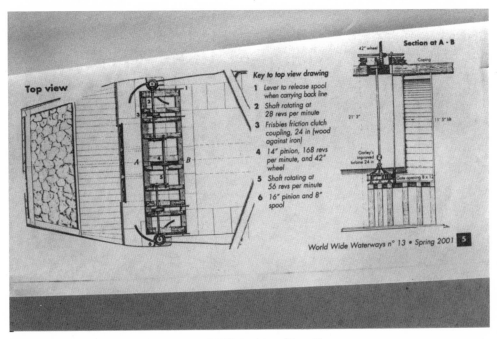

Machinery - Turbine - Superior view - NYS Archives Tom Grasso

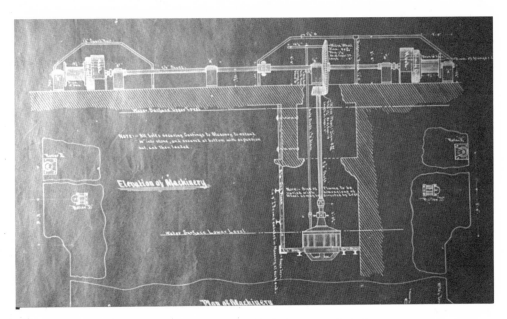

Side view of turbine - Garley's improved 24 inch turbine - NYS Archives

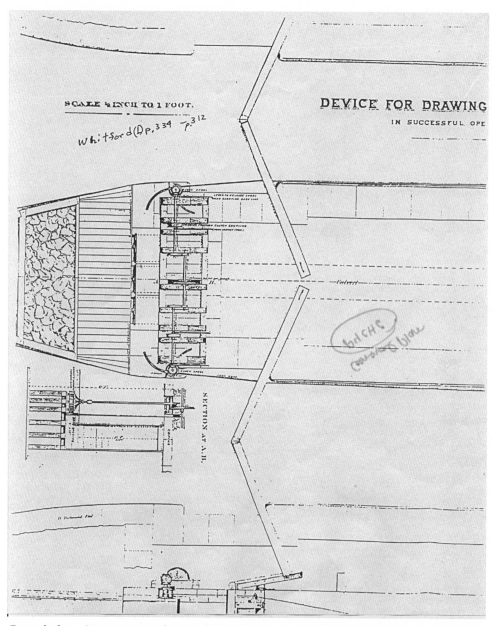

General plan - Lines were used around these drums to move boats into and out of locks. At Lock no. 51, in Jordan, New York, a second drum was situated in the berme middle lock recess powered by an cable or chain.

Sockets, used to support the end of shaft and spool - Lock No. 51 author's collection (G)

Actual lantern from Jordan Lock No. 52. Photo shows the bell used at the Jordan dry dock to warn neighbors prior to the release of water from the dry dock into Skaneateles Creek. Displayed in the Jordan Museum. photo by author - 1985

Head of Lock No. 51. Note twin trees around lock shanty and dog on lock gate walkway. c. 1890 OHA (# 45)

Jordan lock machinery - Campbell's store at Lock No. 51

Close-up of lock machinery, Lock 51 Jordan, New York

This is also viewed at Lock no. 52 in Port Byron. Head of lock

It is interesting to note, that in this middle recess slot at Lock no. 51, there is a water - drain slot chiseled into the outside edge of the stone. This middle recess pivot was held in place with strap irons.

The Garley's 24 inch horizontal improved turbine was powered by excess water dropping through a 8 by 12 inch gate thus turning the turbine.

At Gere's Lock, we have uncovered the wooden platform that supported the Garley's Turbine. The lock pit was filled in, and in the fall of 2003 we continued to remove approximately 8 feet of fill under the platform to clear the mouth of the exit tunnel. On our first excavation trip, we removed large limestone blocks that were pushed into the overflow pit. The largest weighed approximately 3,000 pounds. We believe the reason the pit was filled in was to prevent anyone from falling into the void and injuring themselves. Today, lock stones should not be removed or portions pushed into the chambers, but the lock chambers could be filled with soil which could be removed at a later time. Fencing is also another choice. I happened to be standing on the wooden turbine support floor looking at the keystone portion of the overflow tunnel. I asked the workers (and friends) if they would call the emergency number on their cell phones if I happened to become stuck in the tunnel. No one could remember the emergency number!

Photo showing the wooden floor.

The second excavation trip which took place on April 3, 2003 was accomplished by digging in the constant rain for three hours. In a short time many of our volunteers were wet to the skin. We worried about hypothermia setting in. We had them return to their vehicles to warm themselves and put on dry clothing. We provided food and warm drinks to keep our body heat up to normal. Bill Winks designed a 55 gal. drum with a harness so the drum could be lifted with the crane from the pit and emptied by tipping the drum. It worked without any problems. We used short handled shovels to fill the drum due to the limited working space. We exchanged places often, and we returned again in the fall of 2003.

Working in the pit - 55 gal. drum on left was lowered and filled with dirt. (#2) Hard rain - photo by author

Removing large limestone block. Author (#3)

Tunnel extended the full length of lock. Note daylight at the end of the tunnel, a distance of over 200 feet. Author (#4)

Exit tunnel Lock 51 Jordan, New York. Exit arch is located at the end of the original berme and towpath lock chambers - author (#5)

All of the turbines were removed at the close of the canal and probably sold for scrap or used elsewhere. It would have been priceless to locate the discarded turbine at the bottom of the pit. The latest excavation which took place on November 22, 2003, did not locate the turbine or shaft. We excavated below the wooden turbine floor down to the limestone floor.

I have always believed that the opening above the vertical turbine shaft was covered with a limestone block with a hole drilled for the shaft. Later plans stated that "this hole was to be covered with a 2 1/2 inch oak plank."

There was another method approved by the Superintendent of Public Works to move boats down the locks faster. One or more of the paddle valves were opened creating a flow or current to 'flush' the boat(s) out of the lock. (Whitford - p. 334) "The application of water-power by means of a turbine wheel operating a towing hawser seems to have been in successful operation at Lock No. 52. By the aid of this mechanism boats were drawn into the lock at increased speed and time was saved." (Whitford-p.312)

In 1887 Frick's patented plan of "double headers" which meant one boat coupled behind the other. The "double header" could be pulled by one mule team and haul two loads instead of one. When the boats arrived at a lock, the two boats had to be detached and would lock through separately. In 1884, Gere Lock, No. 50, was to be lengthened at the foot of the lock by extending the berme chamber.

"The improvement consists, in doubling the length of the lock chamber, by taking down the walls of the lock as far as the hollow quoins either at the upper or lower ends... and thence constructing new chamber walls on suitable timber and pile foundations to double the length of the old lock. The old quoins and gates remain so that the lock may be economically used for elevating either one or two boats." (R. Wright - 87 EG) The first lock to be lengthened was Lock No. 50 in 1885: the last was #21 and #22 in 1897. Thirty of the Erie's 72 locks were not lengthened. One of the very rare errors in Whitford's History is the indication (2:1106) that locks No. 36 to No. 39 at Little Falls were lengthened. Contracts were let, but the work was never done. (Taken from field notes written by Richard Wright)

In all of the locks, the exit tunnel ran through the exact center of the island between the lock chambers. At Gere Lock the exit tunnel was extended through the lengthened structure. A wooden pier covers the three entrance portals and the exit tunnel at the foot of the lock of the 46 Enlarged Erie locks that were lengthened, only four were done at the head of the lock. Twenty-six of the First Enlargement locks were not lengthened. (Whitford - p. 1105, Vol. II) The exit tunnel was extended through the lengthened structure. The tunnel at Lock 51 in Jordan was not extended and the end remained between the original lock chambers. The backside of the lengthened berme chamber was not completed in limestone. Many locks, as was Gere's Lock, were completed with a planked platform brought up to the level of the masonry of the berme chamber extension. Lock 56 in Lyons, New York, has a limestone finished backing to the berme lengthened chamber.

Gere Lock was narrower than most of the other locks and built in a swampy area. I feel that the engineers decided it was easier to extend the exit tunnel the full length of the lock instead of leaving the tunnel where it usually ends at the end of a typical set of double locks. The Gere Lock width is 29 ft. 1 inch and the Jordan lock is 30 ft. 11 inches. Remember that three courses of stone, measuring 53 feet 1/2 inch in height, have been removed from the lock and pushed into both lock chambers. The measurement had to be taken at this lower level. Since the lock chamber walls are slightly tapered, the actual pier width at Gere's Lock will be less that the 29 feet 1 inch figure.

The following story is in reference to an exploration trip to the five combines on the Black River Canal. With two companions, I used ropes and a ladder to lower myself into the deep combine locks in order to study their construction. I stated that, "This is crazy. We must be nuts to go to all this trouble to view a lock up close!" My two friends, who were on the top of the lock looking down said, " What do you mean? You are the only one down inside the lock!"

Head of Lock 52, Port Byron, looking northwest - post card - author (D)

Overflow portals Lock No. 52 - Port Byron - Mike Riley is in the left portal - author (D)

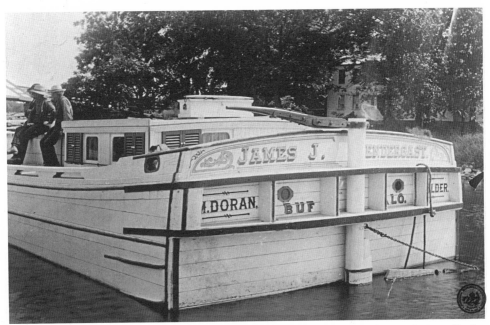

The James J. Pendergast was built by M. Doran, from Buffalo, New York. Gere's Farm Bridge #110 with a rare view of the Gere Homestead on the right. Note the mule evener with a quick release snap on the deck box. OHA #46

Tumble-Gates

In 1871, Heath tumble-gates were used in some locks. The tumble-gate replaced the beam-gate usually on the berme side at the head of the lock. The lock operator could raise and lower the tumble-gate from the island without crossing the lock chamber as he had to do to operate the balance beam in order to open the miter-gate. The balance beam was 27 feet in length.

In 1872, Locks no. 47 and 48 in Syracuse, New York, were fitted with the Heath's "tumble-gate". The tumble gate leaked less water than the miter gates. Gere Lock was not altered to accept the tumble-gate. The first tumble-gate was installed on Lock No. 39 in 1865. It was noted in Whitford p.967, that Heath's patent "tumble-gates," placed in some of the locks, give general satisfaction."

The tumble-gate valves were horizontal and opened and closed from the side wall of the island. Two excellent examples can be seen at Lock 53 in Clyde, New York and Lock 56 in Lyons. A pivoted round timber (i.e.; a horizontal hollow quoin post) rested on the bottom with the gate raising from the head of the lock. The side walls had to be modified to accommodate the tumble-gate. The hollow quoins in the original limestone were removed and square edge stones were placed to provide a seal when the gate was in the upright position. I must include the following excellent description from the Canal Commissioner's report of 1865, p. 29, which will give a better understanding as to the operation of the tumble gate.

"A "tumble gate" has been put in at the head of lock thirty-nine in place of the old mitre gates. It opens up stream by dropping down into the lock below the breast wall, so that boats pass over it. It is hung upon cast-iron journals on a wooden quoin post with sockets let into the lock walls, and turns upon a wooden hollow quoin laid horizontally across the lock. The gate is loaded with stone so that it sinks quickly and is raised by chains connected with gearing at the side of the lock. The mitre sill wall is entirely removed and an open frame work of timber substituted, upon which the hollow quoin rests. A platform extends from the hollow quoin to the breast wall supporting the valves, which are placed horizontally. The valves, though laying horizontally, are worked in a manner similar to the old valves, but from the sidewall of the lock and not from the gate, as was the former practice."

Note: Whitford 1905 uses the English spelling of mitre, while the most common spelling is miter.

The following is paraphrased from the same 1865 report. The horizontal valves allow water to enter the lock chamber with less surge than the vertical miter gates. The simple set of machinery for the raising of the gates could be tended by one man whereas the old gates required two men. The tumble gates were less expensive to install and maintain than the vertical miter gates. White oak and hemlock timbers were used as 2,500 pounds of wrought iron and 320 bounds of cast iron.

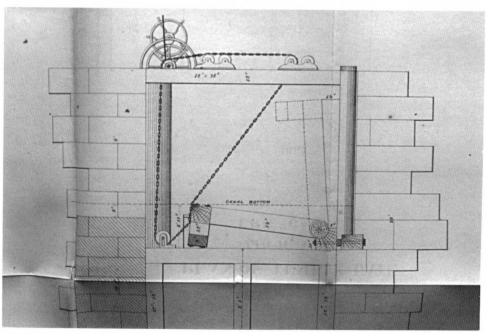

Tumble gate in operation - from CSNYS guide book - NYS Archives.

Tumble-gate in operation - from CSNYS field guide.

Windlass from Waterloo Village Museum is on left and on right is windlass from Sims' Museum - author

Tumble gate recess on Black River Canal at Delta - author

Slot on first enlargement Lock No. 52, Port Byron, New York - author

Slots measuring approximately eight inches wide and three inches deep, were cut in the lock wall approach above the miter gates at the head of the lock. These rough cut slots were used to hold timbers across the lock chamber entrances in order to seal off the lock gates for dry repairs. The Barge Canal today uses the same method. They use a buffer beam across the chamber and vertical corrugated pilings to isolate the lock gates.

Lock Irons

Lock irons were installed above the limestone hollow quoin to provide an adjustable strap to move the wooden hollow quoin post closer to the hollow quoin to take up the slack due to wear. The wooden hollow quoin post must be tight against the curved stone in order to minimize water leakage. The hollow quoin post was fitted with a recessed iron socket at the bottom. This socket was set over a iron pivot fastened to the miter-sill. The triangular miter-sill is raised to allow the miter gate to close and seal against it.

Lock Irons - Mud Lock No. 5 on the Oswego Canal - reconstructed in the 1930's - author (H). Adjustable when hollow quoin post wore.

Lock Irons - Glens Falls feeder 1995 - author (I)

Paddle gate valves were installed at the bottom of the miter gates and could be pivoted by the control rods located at the top of the gate. The valve is pictured in Beardslee's Plan of Composite Valve for Enlarged Locks 1859. (see sketch) The pivotal valve measured 48 inches by 30 inches and was constructed of wrought iron (30 lbs.) and cast iron (165 lbs.) with a wooden core. Throw levers were used to pivot the valve mounted on the side of the balance beam with a walkway positioned on the side of the beam. A set of throw levers was located on each gate along side the balance beam and when they were moved vertically, the valve pivoted through a knuckle connector.

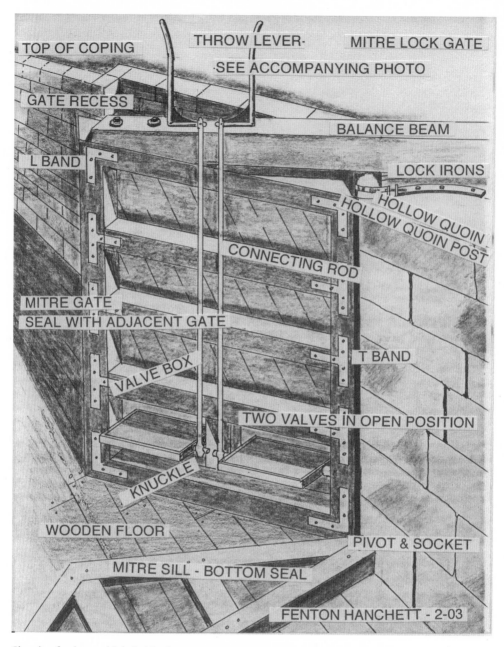

TOP OF COPING

THROW LEVER·
·SEE ACCOMPANYING PHOTO

MITRE LOCK GATE

GATE RECESS

BALANCE BEAM

L BAND

LOCK IRONS

HOLLOW QUOIN

HOLLOW QUOIN POST

CONNECTING ROD

MITRE GATE
SEAL WITH ADJACENT GATE

T BAND

VALVE BOX

TWO VALVES IN OPEN POSITION

KNUCKLE

WOODEN FLOOR

PIVOT & SOCKET

MITRE SILL - BOTTOM SEAL

FENTON HANCHETT - 2-03

Sketch of valve and labeled lock gate parts - Fenton Hanchett, Feb. 8, 2003

110

Figure 7.   55   Drawing of lower berme gate for Enlarged Erie Lock 50, c.1880 (New York State Archives).

Plan of lower berme gate, Lock No. 50 - NYS archives - The hollow quoin post is 17 feet 8 inches high. The valve openings are 4 ft. 1/2 in. wide by 2 ft. 6 in. high. The gate is approximately 11 ft. 6 in. wide.

Socket and pivot - author

Throw lever from our CSNYS collection - author

Throw levers - Champlain Canal - 1995 - author (C)

Cleats to aid in pushing balance beam and open gate - Two examples from Newark Lock No. 59 - author (E)

By opening the paddle valves, water would flow from the high side to the lower side of the gate. When the water level was equal on both sides of the gates, the balance beams could then be pushed to open the gates. The gates would pivot into the lock wall recesses and would become flush with the lock walls of the chamber.

I always wear crokies or eye-glass holders when working around water. I returned to Gere Lock one Sunday to take photographs. I located an ideal area and noticed a small branch in my camera viewfinder. I reached over and snapped the twig, which in turn knocked my glasses into the waters of the lock. This was one time I had forgotten to wear my favorite crokies. The glasses had fallen, from the full-height approach wall. I could not find any handholds in which to lower myself to search the waters. Remembering there was a 16 foot tow rope in my truck, I attached this to the only small tree that we had not cut the day before. I lowered myself along the stone face with one hand and hung on for dear life with the other. After what seemed hours, I retrieved the glasses and continued taking pictures.

Lock Recess: The lock recess along the chamber walls of all First Enlargement locks provide an exact recess for the lock gate to enter and thus provides a completely flat surface along the chamber walls. This is necessary so that a boat entering or leaving the lock will not damage the lock gate, but will find flush chamber lock walls.

A deeper recess is located at the bottom one-third of the lock recess. This provides space for the protruding gate valves and the opening and closing mechanism.

In Jordan, New York, at Lock No. 51, it is interesting to note that a crude recess was placed, at a later date from the original, at the top of the lock gate recess. This undoubtedly accommodated a thicker gate modification and stone had to be removed to allow the gate to remain flush with the walls. It measured on an average 23 inches by 19 inches with crudely chiseled sloped sides. There are many modifications that were introduced causing individual variations on each lock, for example, the island (area between lock chambers) width varies on many locks.

When the berme chamber on Gere Lock was extended, eventually the middle recess was no longer needed. The middle lock gates were not used due to the use of double-headers using this chamber and by planking in the middle lock recess, this avoided boats being caught in the recess. Timber walls were placed of oak eliminating the lock recess and a oak coping covered the top of the recess. The oak coping measured 10 inches by 18 inches and 11 feet 1/4 inches long. This was part of Contract #14 1897, "Details of Timber Walls for Middle Recesses", NYS Canals Middle Division, Syracuse, NY.

The berme middle lock recess on Lock No. 52 at Port Byron, has a limestone coping covering the recess. In fact, the entire lock has been raised with much finer limestone.

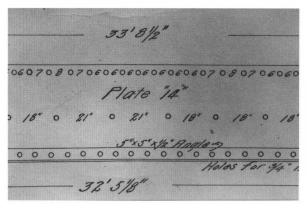

Steel Plates

Steel plates were installed along the berme chamber and the tow-path chamber of Lock No. 50. The plates varied in length with the longest being 26 feet long and 2 feet 5 1/2 inches high. Cast steel hollow quoins were also installed. This would protect the limestone from wear from the boats in the lock chambers.

Steel plates - detail of steel plates - Towpath Chamber, Lock No. 50 Erie Canal. All holes punched for 3/4 inch bolts unless otherwise indicated. Center row of holes is 20 inches from top of plate. NYS Archives

It is interesting to note that steel plates were used as a liner in Gere's Lock. This was under Contract #14 Erie Canal Improvement - Details of Steel Plates for Base of Walls at Lock No. 50. The scale was 1 inch to 4 feet. The contract was approved by the Division Engineer M.H.H. Gere. There were plans also for the Towpath Chamber and Cast Steel Hollow Quoins. The plans stated that All holes punched for 3/4 inch bolts unless otherwise indicated. Rivets were also used. We have discovered that plans may

Gere's Lock excavation showing steel plate bolt heads. These can be seen at the middle of the photo in the wall recess above the floating boards. Nov. 2000 - author.

exist for a project, but the project was never completed. In this case we have a contract number. When we were removing the lock gates at Gere Lock, we made a marvelous discovery. We needed to pump the water out of the lock chamber in order to remove the stones and dirt piled around the gates. Allied Chemical (now Honeywell) used the lock and the canal prism for a water reservoir for the manufacture of chlorine. Allied pumped the water a great distance from a pump house on Nine Mile Creek. The water was used at LCP Chemical Company in making chlorine products. The Solvay plant was closed in 1986. The gates were kept as a barrier to the water and avoided loss of water to the west of the lock. As the water level dropped and as we removed the debris, we located the recess at the bottom of the lock walls which at one time contained the steel plates. The bolt heads were still in place according to the plans, but the plates themselves had been removed for scrap. The plate recesses measured 35 inches high.

The lock gates were in a closed position and acted as a barrier to contain the water in the reservoir. Small round stones and clay surrounded the lock gates to further insure that there was a watertight seal in the water basin.

Since water was no longer being pumped into the canal reservoir, the water level dropped over the years. A decision was made to remove the lock gates before they rotted beyond removal. Wood underwater, deprived of oxygen, will remain preserved. The structure will only decay once it is exposed to the air. The top of the gates, approximately 8 to 9 feet had already decayed to the water line.

We decided to dig out the furthest gate from the berme side of the lock as it was in better condition than the gate on the near side. This began in the summer of 1995. A water pump was used to remove the standing water each time as we dug the stones and clay away from the gate. We had to completely dig out the gate in order to use a crane to lift the gate out of the lock chamber. We could not just pull the gate out of the mud as the suction would be too great and the gate would be pulled apart. We needed to place straps under the lock gate as well as around the gate. As we dug deeper (eventually eight feet) the wet clay would slide toward the pit where we were digging. This created a dangerous situation. Wooden pallets were used to terrace the mud and avoided it sliding on us. The water pump would constantly plug with snails. We all worked in the mud up to our waist. Mud filled our boots and clothing. We had food delivered, and even though we rinsed out hands, the food tasted like mud. It was a great learning experience!

It took four sessions to dig out the lock. It was smelly, dirty work. We wonder where we find volunteers that enjoy doing this type of work! I was asked to place the straps around the gate. If it fell apart, it was on my head. With the tremendous assistance from the Town of Camillus providing heavy equipment, Bill Winks, the main operator, plus many volunteers, the gate was lifted out of the chamber. The gate was suspended on straps from the boom and carried up the berme to the parking lot and loaded onto a trailer to be transported to the Camillus Erie Canal Park.

Lock No. 50 south chamber - 1897-98 - Note the man at the lower right holding the steel sheeting. OHA (#7)

Lock excavation in 1997 of lock gates - author (J)

Workers after working in the mud - author (K)

Lifting the lock gate - 1997 - author (L)

On site at Sims' - Two photos showing the repositioned lock gate and a close-up of the valve. - author

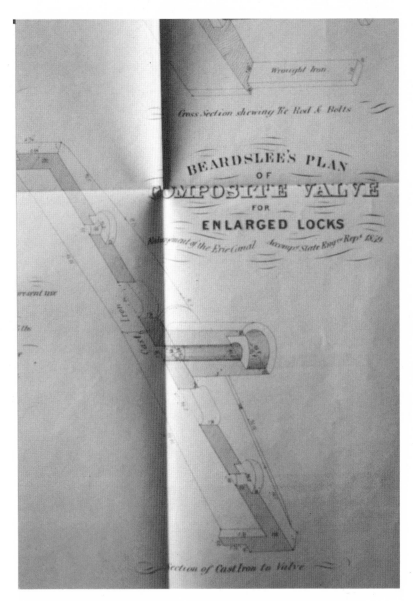

Beardslee's plan for composite valve for enlarged locks - NYS Archives. Shows knuckle for opening gate when throw rods were thrown pivoting the valve.

MITER SILL - new construction in preparation to position the lock gates against the miter sill. The miter sills were originally constructed of solid timbers. Due to cost, we laminated hemlock boards together to form the miter sill. - author

Preservation - One method of stabilizing the wood would be to send the gate to a facility and preserve it using polyethylene glycol. This would be too expensive. There are other methods of wood preservation. We decided to use Olympic Wood Protector on the wood and Enrust on the wrought iron.

The decision was made to remove only one lock gate and attempt preservation. If this did not attain our goal, then we still had a second gate in water at the lock. The lock gate has been sprayed four times a year, and we are happy to report that the wood is stable and shown no signs of deterioration. We then removed the second gate in the year 2000. We have built an outdoor, roofed exhibit to show the lock gates with their miters together in position and against a newly constructed miter sill.

The round hollow-quoin post sat into the stone hollow quoin and provided a seal. The miter sill was a seal for the bottom of the gates. The bevel or miter when the lock gates came together also provided a seal. We have a "U" shaped seal on each lock gate. The gates can be adjusted to a limited degree by the lock iron adjustments.

A stop gate was installed to the east of Gere's Lock No. 50, as failure of this lock would cause water to flow into the City from Jordan, New York. The stop gate was placed in 1874 as noted in the Annual Report of the Canal Commissioners at a cost of $138.10. The stop gate was repaired in 1895.

There was great concern that if the lower lock gate of Lock 47 gave way, tremendous and disastrous flooding would occur in the City of Syracuse. There was a long level extending from Rome west to Lock 47 in the City of Syracuse. Locks 47, 48 and 49 locked down to the west in Syracuse meaning that the waters from Lock 46 in Utica and Lock 50 in Geddes would all flow to the lowest point which was Syracuse. The many feeders would also flow unimpeded to the lowest level. The lock gates were kept in good condition and inspected on a regular basis. The Superintendent of Public Works in the Annual Report of 1881 recommended the keeping of two men constantly on each of Locks 47,48 and 49.

The State of New York installed two stop gates. There was a tumble gate facing east installed to the east of Syracuse in 1886. It is described in Assembly Document of 1888. It was made of strong construction of over 40 feet in length and lies below the bottom of the canal. It was counterweighted so it could be released easily with machinery arranged for this purpose. Three self-adjusting braces caused it to form a strong bulk-head. A bulkhead with gates, for feeding purposes, connected with it on the berme side. Cut stone abutments with vertical end walls and pile fenders were also placed. The location was at the west end of the Rome level, and just above the wide waters and high embankments at the head of Lock 47.

The level of the canal waters to the east was 25 feet above the streets of Syracuse. The State had timbers and planks with which to form a dam across the trunk at Butternut Creek Aqueduct 5 miles from Syracuse. This would take time to implement and much damage would be done to the City. (Ass. Doc. 1888)

The exact location of the stop gate was east of Teall Avenue between Ives and Barnstable. There was also concern of leakage of the twin New York Central railroad tunnels under the Erie Canal east of Lock 47. The tunnels have been filled in and the coping of the south portal is present today along Erie Boulevard East.

The number of lockages occurring at Lock 50 in 1881 was 19,775. The number of lockages in 1895 was 16, 681. It is interesting to note that the Superintendent's salary for section no. 6 was $1500.00 yearly in 1895.

POST CARD - tunnel on the N.Y.C.R.R. Syracuse, New York. The twin tunnels ran under the Erie Canal First Enlargement - author

Cement coping over the twin tunnels on Erie Boulevard East between Teall Avenue and Beach Street - 2002 - author

Staples which held the limestone blocks from moving - Holes are drilled into the stone and lead is poured around the staple to hold it in place. - author

The remains of the Geddes Pump House located to the east of Gere Lock. The photo shows the canal water supply pipe that powered the pumps. There were three brine pump houses around the east end of Onondaga Lake. There is an intact wooden floor under the standing water. The following is of interest taken from the NYS Engineer and Surveyors Report of 1854. "To obtain a permanent and increased supply of water for the summit level extending from Lock No. 50 to Lock No. 51, resort may be had to Otisco Lake. By converting this lake to a reservoir, an abundant supply of water could be obtained for the canal westward from Syracuse to Clyde, and also for driving the public pumps at the salt springs on the Syracuse level. A resurvey and estimate has been ordered."

OHA - Boys on towpath - Looking east from below Lock No. 50-Note listed Leo Semlik? Note the boy on the left, the absence of his left leg. Looking toward Solvay, New York (#58)

Chapter 7

Culverts ~ Clinton's Ditch and First Enlargement

Clinton's Ditch

Culverts are remarkable structures which basically collect the run-off water from the higher hillsides and streams plus the 'State Blue-Line ditches' and distribute the excess water into a lower stream or river. The culverts carry floods and freshets away from the vulnerable banks. The State ditches run parallel to the towpath and berme diverting water from possible washing out the banks. The hillside water is collected at the high side and transported underneath the canal prism in culverts to the other side of the canal. In the middle division, construction is provided for eight large culverts, of stone, and fifteen smaller ones of iron: and there are thirteen aqueducts , which necessarily leave capacious water-courses beneath them. There are seventeen waste-weirs. A waste-weir discharges excess water within the canal. (p. 411 - Canal Laws-Vol.1) A waste-weir is a pre-set overflow structure removing excess water from the canal. The spillway can be located along the canal banks or part of the aqueduct structure.

The following descriptions are taken from Canal Terminology of the United States by Hahn and Kemp.

Waste weir: a stone, concrete, or wooden structure built in the towpath bank of the canal with gates or stop planks, the lifting of which enabled the draining of a level of a canal for repairs, cleaning, or protection from ice in winter.

Spillway: a device built in, or at, the river side of the towpath to carry off excess water caused by rain or the improper control of the water in the level at the lock downstream. Also, an overflow. Sometimes, used to describe the bypass flume at the side of the lock. A passageway in, around, or over a dam to release the water upstream.

Water that flows into the culverts is not diverted into the canal, except in the case of a stream receiver i.e. Carpenter's Brook waste-weir at Peru, N.Y., to provide an additional amount of water, because it would cause silting and a current that the mules would have to pull against.

There is no substitute for actual field work. On a bright Sunday summer morning, I was exploring the remains of the Salina sidecut which parallels Hiawatha Boulevard near the Regional Market. I was standing in the middle of a small lot when I noticed a large sign directly behind me. It stated, "NO TRESPASSING FOR ANY REASON." I am usually unaware of such notices. At that exact moment, a City of Syracuse policemen slowly drove past the lot. I waved to him, and he acknowledged me with a wave and continued on his way—A moment in time!

First Enlargement

There were berme marker stones on the First Enlargement, set in concrete, directly above the culvert. These were used as a marker warning dredging crews to avoid the culvert roof which was part of the prism floor. We believe that there was a faceted hole located in the middle of the culvert on the prism floor. We further believe there was a plug with perhaps a steel ring in the top that acted as a plug or stopper. Tom Grasso, President of the Canal Society of New York State , remembers seeing such a plug discarded in the culvert in Montezuma, N. Y. A chain perhaps was attached to the ring and placed around the berme marking stone for easier removal of the plug. Further field study must be made to ascertain the plug's existence. State of New York culvert plans do not show the existence of such a plug. The drain plug, if it existed, would allow the complete drainage of a section of the canal through the top of the culvert. One may be able to enter such an intact culvert to determine its actual composition.

Mike Riley, a Camillus Canal Society Board member, and I crawled into a nearby culvert to see if we could locate the culvert plug that was used for draining the canal through the top of the culvert. It was winter time and the ice was in a semi-firm state, but not very deep. The ice cracked often, and when we reached the center of the culvert, we were unable to see any plug. The interior of the culvert had been relined in cement, and the features of the stone were impossible to ascertain. Mike asked me what would happen if we got stuck inside the culvert. The cell phone may not work. I mentioned that my truck was parked on the little-used highway, and eventually someone would locate us. This increased his anxiety level.

Berme marking stones - two examples - author

Culvert marking stones that I have measured, are not uniform in dimensions. The culvert marking stone east of Weedsport measures 17 1/2 inches high (above current ground level which would fill in with soil and debris), 21 inches wide and 8 1/2 inches thick. The culvert marking stone at MacDonald Road in Elbridge measures 23 inches exposed above ground, 29 inches wide and 9 1/2 inches thick.

Most of these stones observed have been set in a ball of concrete to stabilize them.

White Bottom Brook marking stone in cement - author - marking stone and cement ball pushed into canal and lying on its side. 2003

White Bottom Brook culvert

I have noted that it is unfortunate these culvert stones, culverts, and most aqueducts, locks and spillways were not inscribed with a builders mark or a date. (See chapter 18) A road culvert was constructed at Medina, New York. Two cornerstones were placed at both ends of this culvert in 1823 under Clinton's Ditch. One cornerstone (now in the Camillus Sims' Store Museum and owned by the CSNYS) lists the Canal Commissioners. Please see chapter 10 for the actual description. The names of the builders and architect are inscribed in the second stone, which is in the foundation of the Toussaint home on Culvert Road.

There were basically five types of culvert construction:

1. Cast iron
2. Stone
3. Composite - constructed of wood and stone.
4. Wood
5. Brick & concrete or stone

Many of the earlier Clinton's Ditch culverts were made of cast iron. The iron culverts consist of cast pieces in the shape of half cylinders with flanges connected together with nuts and bolts.

Cast iron culvert at Rome Village - author

Smaller cast iron drain culvert pipe - Rome Village - author

The Ditch cast iron culverts were contracted at the rate of $80 per ton delivered. The iron culverts, three feet in diameter cost about $500 secured at the site. Those two feet in diameter cost about $340, and culverts one foot in diameter cost about $170. In the middle division the culvert length varied between 60 and 75 feet.

The specifications for these iron culverts call for "good iron, smooth and even, with all their edges and ends so shaped so that they may fit close together when they are laid in the culverts." The pieces are to be in the form of half cylinders three eights of an inch in thickness or more and not less than three feet in length. Culvert pieces may be less than three feet when completing the ends of the culvert. (Canal Laws - Vol.1 - p. 419)

Cast iron culvert pipes were used at White Bottom Brook #60 and many other locations on the First Enlargement. The culvert consists of three segmented iron pipes each 129 feet long with each pipe having a span of three feet and three feet high. Water was drained from the canal between Camillus and Jordan after the canal ceased operation. The First Enlargement was officially closed in 1917, but sections of the canal were used for local use until about 1922 when Syracuse's Clinton's Square area was starting to be filled in. The canal was drained west of Memphis, New York, White Bottom Brook, and the Carpenter's culvert and spillway. The story, according to Walt Zelie, the head of the Carpenter's Brook Fish Hatchery in Elbridge, stated that dynamite was floated into the middle of the cast iron pipes and the explosion opened the pipes causing the water to drain into the creeks. One pipe was destroyed at White Bottom Creek and two pipes were destroyed at the Carpenter's Brook Culvert. I am undergoing a study regarding the feasibility of restoring water to this section of the canal. The Carpenter's Brook spillway can be restored by replacing several limestone blocks that remain on site. Wooden timbers can be reintroduced to hold the water back and some of the wooden flooring would have to be replaced.

Smaller cast iron drain pipe - Camillus - author.

Ditch stone culverts: The limestone used varied in cost from 75 cents to $1.37 per ton according to circumstances. There are inexhaustible quantities of lime and sandstone within eight miles of the sites. The prices include the purchasing, quarrying and delivering of large, thick, solid, durable, and well faced stone.

Stone was purchased by weight and not by the cord or perch (a solid measure for stone, commonly 16 1/2 feet by 1 1/2 feet by 1 foot) as this lessens the temptation of contractors to alter them for their use, by breaking them up into small pieces. This would make them easier to handle, and it would also increase their measurement. It was just as easy to weigh the stone as opposed to piling them up for measuring.

The stone culverts vary in length from 64 feet to 120 feet at Hughes's Creek. (Canal Laws - p. 419)

Holley Ditch culvert - author

First Enlargement culverts: The following is according to the Canal Commissioner Report and the State Engineer Reports of 1852-54.

"All culverts are to be built upon timber and plank foundations except where rock occurs of sufficient solidity and durability to support the structure permanently. Ten of the small culverts with three-feet openings, are to have side and end-walls of cement masonry, and a covering of timber and plank. Culverts with openings exceeding three feet in width, to have semi-circular arches and such height of jamb walls as may be adapted to their location. The masonry to be of good durable stone and so dressed that the horizontal joins of face and arch work will not exceed a quarter of an inch."

The above description is accurately recorded. Culvert No. 59 (number only) is located in our Town Canal Park and is an arched culvert consisting entirely of stone on a wooden base. The culvert is 135 feet long with a single arch with an opening four feet wide and two feet six inches high.

Culvert 59 - author

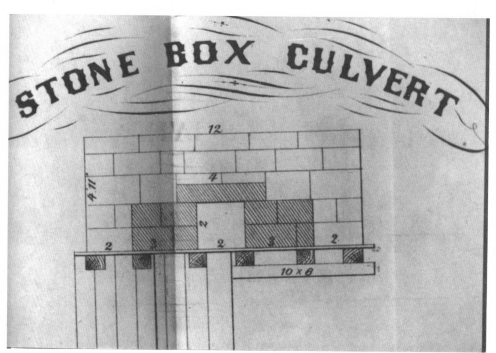

Culvert plans - NYS Archives - author

Shearer's Culvert - author

The Shearer's culvert located immediately to the West of Jordan Lock 51 is a composite culvert and shows marked signs of deterioration. It has one opening 120 feet 10 inches in length with a span of four feet and a height of two feet.

There are well over 300 culverts listed in detail in Whitford Vol. Two. Some of the culverts list parts a and b as well as extra culverts for sewage.

Geddes Culvert #56 viewed from the north side and has two openings 124 feet long with a span of 4 feet and a height of 3 feet - Designated as a fish ladder in Geddes Brook. (# 28) OHA

Chapter 8

LOCK SHANTIES

The Camillus Erie Canal volunteers have created a very unique structure. We constructed a replica of a lock tender's shanty in Jordan, and it is similar to the one that once stood on the center island or pier at Gere's Lock No. 50 in Camillus, New York. Mrs. Francis Berlinski, deceased, remembered many details of the Gere's Lock shanty which was situated across from her home on Belle Isle Road. On the First Enlargement the lock shanty was located between the lock chambers. This gave the lock tender, when not busy, an opportunity to sit down, fill out reports and still be able to see the approaching canal boats. The lock master and his family usually lived within walking distance of the lock in a larger lock house.

On one of my many exploration trips, I noticed an abandoned building in a badly decomposed state to the north of Jordan Lock No. 51. This building proved to be the original lock shanty that was once positioned between the lock chambers on the central pier. My main concern was increased vandalism and the possibility of fire. I approached the Village of Jordan officials and found little interest in the preservation of this structure.

We continued our efforts to save the shanty, and we obtained a trailer from a friend. He would be able to move the shanty on a flat bed trailer to Camillus. We set a date for this move in the hope that Jordan would claim this prize and restore it. We would rather reproduce such a structure in Camillus even though it would not be original. Jordan came to the rescue, and said they would move the building and restore it. We compliment them on preserving this rare structure.

Replica of lock shanty completed. The original did not have a rain cap over the chimney.

137

The Jordan lock house was moved from the pier between the berme and towpath chambers to a semi-level site to the north of the towpath. We were not able to ascertain how the lock house was moved across the towpath chamber or when it was moved. A Mr. Louis Kabusla lived in the lock shanty for many years prior to his death circa, 1972. He shared his time between living at the State School on Wilbur Avenue and the Jordan lock house. He paid $5.00 a year to the State of New York and $5.00 to the Village of Jordan for yearly rent. Neither parties could determine the ownership of the structure at that time.

Another story, relating to Mr. Kabusla, was told to me by my colleague, Harry T. Sweeney, DDS, whose father was the owner of the Jordan Hotel. In order not to offend his patients, Dr. Whitley, a local physician, examined Mr. Kabusla immediately in his office. Mr. Kabusla did not bath very often. Mr. Kabusla would be considered a hermit by today's standards. He died at the age of 65 in the lock shanty.

Frank Bunce and I measured and photographed the lock shanty, and it was accurately reproduced at our Camillus Erie Canal Park. The Jordan structure measured 10 feet by 12 feet with low window sills facing east and west. The door swung inward and faced north toward the towpath. The pot bellied stove was three feet from the west window and a coal-coke box was along the back wall. The original chimney built of bricks and mortar, was suspended two feet below the ceiling supported on metal brackets. The brick chimney extended through the air space between the ceiling and the underside of the roof. The original chimney did not have a rain cap in place to prevent water from entering the chimney. The wood stove pipe extended from the stove and entered the chimney at the front with a bend of 90 degrees. The box measured approximately 6 feet long by 3 feet high and was 3 feet wide with a hinged lid. Between lockings the lock tender would pull a blanket from the box and sleep on the top of it. There were also two chairs inside and, perhaps, a small table.

In restoring the lock shanty we had two volunteers that were willing to use lath plaster for the walls. Originally, horse hair strands were used to reinforce the plaster placed over the wooden lath boards. Since horse hair was no longer available, the two men obtained plaster containing fiber glass as a binder. For many years the walls have retained their original appearance without cracking.

One of the Camillus lock tenders was Mr. Bankey. He and his family lived in North Belle Isle. A kerosene lantern positioned at each end of the island or pier, mounted on a post and protected in glass from the wind, provided a beacon for the boats locking through at night. Night lockings were discontinued in the 1880's.

A working photo of the Jordan lock shanty. Note that the mule shoe is nailed upside down allowing the "luck" to run out. OHA photo

Jordan lock shanty moved beyond the towpath to the north. Exterior views -author

Interior of Jordan lock shanty. Photo taken of one corner of shanty showing wallpaper, window on left, door on right and debris on floor - author.

Below - Sketch of lock shanty in Jordan - by Frank Bunce. The dimensions of the shanty are 10 feet by 12 feet

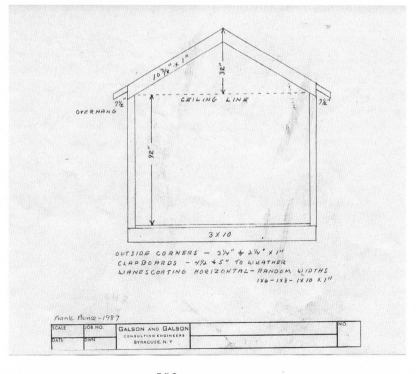

10 3/8" x 1"   32"

7 1/2"   CEILING LINE   7 1/2"

OVERHANG

92"

3 X 10

OUTSIDE CORNERS — 3 1/4" & 2 1/4" X 1"
CLAPBOARDS — 4 1/2 & 5" TO WEATHER
WANESCOATING HORIZONTAL—RANDOM WIDTHS
1X6 — 1X8 — 1X10 X 1"

Frank Bunce —1987

SCALE	JOB NO.	GALSON AND GALSON		NO.
DATE	OWN.	CONSULTING ENGINEERS SYRACUSE, N.Y		

Our Gere Lock site in Camillus has been modified appreciably as we discussed in the Gere Lock chapter. The pier between the chambers on Lock 51 in Jordan, New York yielded a great amount of information. In the middle of the island, I noticed five depressions in the soil. The four rectangularly positioned outermost holes represent the four foundations for the four posts or stone columns that supported the corners of the lock shanty. The fifth depression was located to the side of the lock shanty between the cast-iron stove and the rear wall. This fifth depression was for the removal of the "potty" bucket from the outside.

Jordan lock shanty north of towpath showing the front entrance. - author

Interiors of Various Lock Shanties

The Jordan group that moved and restored the Jordan lock shanty, located a toilet hole in the floor. This would enable the lock tender to use this facility inside the lock house.

Lock shanty windows were lower than a normal house window. While he was seated, this would enable the lock tender to see approaching boats from either direction. There was one brass and one tin card holder, each measuring 7 1/4 inches by 10 3/4 inches in the Jordan lock shanty. The tin holder was located to the left behind the door.

Jordan lock shanty after being moved to the DPW site.

Lock shanty restored and moved to canal site in front of Ramsdell School.

The second holder of brass was located to the right of the window. We will attempt to determine what type of information, i.e.: schedules, were inserted in these holders. The card was inserted from the top.

Each lock shanty contained a brick supported internal chimney stack near the ceiling. The heavy brick-lined, tile insert is connected to the roof chimney. The brick chimney is supported by 3/4 inch threaded rods from the ceiling supports.

Jordan chimney support

Camillus replica chimney

A lock shanty has been placed on the north side of Lockville Lock No. 59. John Hatch and Joe Donovan of the Canal Corporation in Lyons, New York, believe that the lock shanty originally was located on Lock No. 4, of the Cayuga-Seneca Canal in Waterloo, New York. - author

The small 10 foot by 12 foot lock - house could be very adequately heated using a small wood stove. The usual box cast iron stove sat on a insulated medium such as a brick base with tin underneath to avoid excessive heat to the wooden floor. The stove pipe connected the stove with a recess placed in the heavy brick support inner chimney.

The center pier at the Upper Lockville Lock No. 59 (now Newark, N.Y.) contains a stone step that led to the original lock shanty. author

144

The old lock, looking North on the Cayuga-Seneca Canal, Cayuga, N.Y. Note the different style of lock shanty. Postcard. - author

Lock No. 53 Clyde, New York, "Sunset at the Lock" with a 4.63 foot lift west. The roof line was orientated north-south with the door opening facing east. The windows usually faced the head and foot of the lock so that the lock tender could see the approaching boats. Postcard - author

Tin horns and conch shells were used to signal the lock tender of the boats approaching the lock at night. All of the boats hung reflective lanterns on the bow cabin to help see the towpath, and the lock tender could easily see the lighted boat approaching. A single lamp meant a single tow; two lights meant a double tow and that the enlarged berme chamber needed to be use.

The lock shanty door (usually solid in construction) faced most often the towpath chamber. The door at Gere Lock No. 50 and Jordan Lock No. 51 faced to the north, or the towpath chamber. The roof orientation of the lock shanty is very interesting. A photo taken in 1896 showed the peak of the roof running parallel with the lock chambers. In an abandonment photo, circa 1930, the new lock shanty roof peak ran north-south or at right angles to the lock chambers.

The following observations were taken from the Gayer collection of photos Number I to XIV. The door faced the end of the lock chambers at Lock No. 1. The Gere lock house was painted a light color, probably white, with a darker color on the 4 inch border molding. The later abandonment photo does not show any color contrast. Most of the lock houses from Lock No. 1 at Waterford to Lock 56 at Lyons, New York, were basically similar.

Some of the lock houses had small frames above the windows showing the number of the lock. Gere Lock No. 50 and the Jordan Lock No. 51 had the "Lock No. 50" and "Lock No. 51" painted over the windows.

Lock No. 32, First Enlargement, Erie Canal at Fort Plain, New York. This lock had a lift of 7.759 feet to the west. The lock shanty roof line is parallel to the lock chambers. Postcard - author

146

A view of the lock shanty from the foot of Lock 52. Postcard - author

PHOTO - shows two views of the lock shanty from the head and foot of Lock 52. Postcards - author (Above image is foot of Lock 52)

A view of the lock shanty from the head of Lock 52. Postcard - author

Lock No. 49 had a single shutter to close over the windows probably to protect the windows in the winter months. Gere Lock did not show shutters in any of the photos viewed. We have placed double shutters on our replica of our lock house to prevent vandalism. We have also placed a slate stone over the chimney to prevent rain from entering the chimney.

Craig Williams provided me with a list of lock shanties and to whom they were sold. The Lock Berlin lock shanty was sold and moved to a nearby cemetery behind the Methodist Church in the small village of Lock Berlin. In the middle of the winter of 1991, I attempted to determine whether the lock shanty still existed. I arrived at the cemetery and walked up a slight incline past the church. The wind velocity began to increase and the snow fall was extremely heavy, cutting my visibility to about 20 feet. I passed the church and entered the cemetery and attempted to walk to the very end boundary. As I neared the end of the property, I saw a white silhouette of a small building. As I stumbled closer, the structure was the size and description of a lock shanty, less a chimney. This was indeed an original lock shanty and was included as a stop on one of our Canal Society of New York State field trips. The lock shanty has been moved (1994) to a site North of Newark to be restored by the E.R.I.E. group.

This lock shanty has asbestos lining the chimney. The windows have rotation wooden latches to secure them at any height. The ceiling vent has a pivoting tin cover to prevent the entrance of rain. There is a seat that folds up against the wall. The wall covering was tongue and groove covered with wallpaper. A potty hole was not in evidence. The single door was orientated at the end of the roof peak, with two windows being at a low level.

Lock shanty at cemetery in Lock Berlin

Lock Berlin lock shanty after move to Newark

Above - Collapsible seat

Right - Interior chimney support

We are actively searching for additional surviving lock shanties. The following are the sites of additional known lock shanties:

A lock shanty was located in the yard of a farm to the north of the lower Macedon Lock No. 60. The farmer was using the lock shanty for storage and the structure was in good condition.

Macedon lock shanty

Poorhouse Lock 56: This brick structure located on the south side of the lock may have been used as a store and privately owned. A lock shanty may have been located to the east of the store.

Hinsmanville lock shanty. Standing lock shanty (above) - January 2000.
Post card (below) - author - note single-chamber lock

View on Oswego River looking South, Oswego, N. Y.

Craig Williams makes reference to this structure in the Canal Society of New York State field guide on the Oswego Canal, October 14, 1989. Craig states that Lock No. 6 at Hinsmanville is the best preserved lock on the Oswego Canal. As I have mentioned earlier, a stove was provided in the lock shanty as well as a "potty" hole. In the annual report of the Superintendent of Public Works, September 1883, it mentions that a new house was constructed adjacent to the lock which was probably the lock shanty. The lock shanty stood on the river side of the lock and measured 9 feet by 12 feet. Liz and I visited the lock on Jan. 1st, 2003, and much to our sorrow, the lock shanty had fallen completely apart and was lying on the ground.

Two photos of lock shanty - Waterloo - Cayuga-Seneca Canal - located in the DOT (now Canal Corporation) maintenance buildings and used as a paint shop.

The original Waterloo lock house used on the enlarged Cayuga-Seneca Canal was moved to a new site on the north side of the Barge Canal after 1915. It was used as a lock shanty for the Barge Canal at Lock # 4 in Waterloo until it was replaced by a modern building. The original lock building was again relocated in 1960 and moved to the State Department of Canals and Waterways located on the south side of the Barge Canal. It was used as a paint and sign shop when I visited the site in 1989.

Seneca Falls Lock Shanty - Postcard

Caughdenoy Lock House - author

Typical lock house plans - NYS Archives

The State Department of Transportation, which has been taken over by the Canal Corporation, removed all of the newer buildings leaving the original lock shanty in a secure fenced-in area.

The Caughdenoy lock house is a large two story structure located to the south of the now inactive Caughdenoy lock, where the lock master and his family lived. The typical lock house dimensions in 1855 from the NYS Archives, measured 25 feet wide and 34 feet deep.

This was part of the towed section of the Oneida River and not a towpath canal section. There were locks located at Oak Orchard and Caughdenoy on the Oneida River between the Oswego River and Oneida Lake.

Bob Kellogg, one of our active volunteers, now deceased, purchased a house previously owned by a boat captain on the first enlargement. While remodeling, Bob discovered a leather pouch resting on a ceiling beam. It contained many bills of lading which are reproduced and displayed in our lock shanty replica at the Canal Park.

Craig Williams notes that the State instituted in 1902 a system of numbered badges for all "lock-tenders, bridge-tenders and bank watchmen". This was initiated as a mark of respect for the all important duties performed by the State workers. (CSNYS field guide, Oct. 13, 1090 - Eastern Montgomery County, p. I-35)

"The Superintendent of Public Works, each Assistant Superintendent, foreman of sections or lock tender has all the authority of a peace officer with a warrant, to arrest any person engaged in the commission of a crime affecting any of the canals, or any person whom he has reasonable cause to believe has committed such crime; and shall forthwith take the person so arrested before any magistrate of the county within which the crime is committed, to be dealt with according to law." Laws, Rules & Regulations Governing Navigation of the State Canals, Oct. 1929.

Right - Typical boat horn and conch shell used to signal the lock master of an approaching boat. - author.

Boat lantern hung on front of bow cabin. This gave the captain minimum illumination to see the banks and mule team pulling the boat at night. Some lanterns had side reflectors to direct the light. If the lock master saw one light, he knew it was a single tow and would use the single towpath lock chamber. If he saw two lanterns, he knew it was a double tow, and would place the boats in the double, lengthened chamber without having to separate the tow.

Mule bridge - This allowed mules to be "tailed" from the stern mule cabin to the towpath. This photo was taken in 1988 of the mule bridge reproduction at the Canal Museum in Syracuse, N.Y., in their outdoor exhibit. (now removed) - author.

Chapter 9

Bench Marks, Blue Lines and Red Line Monuments

Measuring error - I am no longer allowed to do any of the measuring at the Camillus Erie Canal Park. At the marina , I carefully measured the exact length of our first canal pontoon boat, which is still in service. We were going to store the boat at that time in our garage attached to the Sims' Museum. I measured the inside of the garage and determined with the boat inside, we would have one foot to spare. The day arrived, and the pontoon boat was being moved on its trailer into the garage. I was in the garage carefully watching both sides of the boat so it would not hit the walls. I finally said, "stop!" I observed that the boat was as far into the garage as it would go. A loud voice outside was heard to say, "the boat is still sticking out of the garage by four feet!" They were correct! I had forgotten that we had a bathroom, four foot square, in the middle of the garage and the boat was tight against it. I measured along the wall and had forgotten about it. We had to tear out the bathroom in order for the boat to fit. You make one little mistake, and it follows you forever!

Accurate measurements of distance and height were of vital necessity in designing and surveying the earlier Grand Canal, First Enlargement, and the present Barge Canal.

In 1876, a resurvey of the bench marks was ordered by the State Engineer using "Y" levels which we will describe. Many of the earlier bench marks since 1876, which were placed on stone structures, have disappeared or have been moved when the structures were rebuilt.

These bench marks were resurveyed in 1900 and 1901. Much of this information comes from the pocket edition of "Lists of Spirit Levels and Bench Marks Along New York State Canals" from the annual report for 1901 of Edward A. Bond, State Engineer and Surveyor.

The initial bench-mark of the survey is known as the "Grist Mill" bench at Greenbush (now Rensselaer), New York. This BM was established by the U.S. Coast and Geodetic Survey in 1857. The building on which this BM was placed was in extremely poor structural shape and the BM was moved to the Post Office building in Albany. The cornerstone of the Post Office building was laid in 1879 and is now part of the SUNY system. The metal plaque is located on the southeast corner of the building about five feet off the ground.

Old post office and federal building - 1879-83 - Albany, New York - photo by author - 2003

Metal bench mark plaque - photo by author - 2003

The wording is as follows: United States Department of Agriculture Weather Service Bench Mark No 0 Elevation 25.000 Feet River Service

IN WHITFORD, Vol. 2 states that all elevations in these Tables of Existing Structures on Canals have mean tide at New York as zero of the datum plane, and were derived by using bench marks established by the Barge canal levels of 1901, which started from the "Grist Mill" bench mark at Greenbush (Rensselaer), N.Y. with an elevation of 14.730.

There are interesting distance measurements in the History of New York Canals, 1906, Vol. 2 by Noble E. Whitford. The Tables of Structures on the Erie Canal list measurements "Continuous stations from Hudson river junction". He would list a six digit number after the structure listed.

Example: Lock No. 50 - Gere's Lock 9,062+05 The six-digit numeral is the distance in feet from Hudson River Junction in Albany. A smaller number sometimes will appear below the six-digit number which represents the distance in feet between structures. Station: the distance between stations is 100 feet. This is a measurement and not a point. Multiply 9,062 continuous stations times 100 feet and you arrive at 9,062,00 feet. Add +05 feet, and you arrive at 9,062,05 feet. Divide by 5,280 feet, which is the number of feet in one mile and the distance from the Hudson River junction to Gere's lock is 171.63 miles.

Surveying party - photo of towpath wall at Gere's farm bridge. Note the well-dressed men with ties and hats. Note the horse and buggy under the bridge. OHA (# 2)

Bench marks were established on all locks and all permanent canal structures. Survey parties consisted in 1901 of five men; an instrument man, a recorder, two rodmen and an umbrella man. The latter man shaded the delicate surveying instrument from the sun and during its moving from point to point.

Rodman no. 1 stayed at the bench mark while the instrument man paced off 200 to 225 feet and set-up his instrument. Rodman no. 2 proceeded the same distance beyond the instrument man. The instrument was leveled and the distance was recorded back to rodman no. 1 and then to rodman no. 2. When "all right" was yelled, this procedure was repeated. Steel pins were driven into the ground at an angle to mark the measured distance.

The Pocket Edition of "Lists of Spirit Levels and Bench Marks along New York State Canals" from the Annual Report for 1901 states the essentials for obtaining good results. You must have a good instrument with a sensitive bubble, kept in perfect adjustment. The instrument must have equal back sights and fore sights, and the instrument must be protected from the direct rays of the sun at all times. Work must cease when bad air or wind do not allow two settings of the target on the same point within .002 of a foot. The chief of the party should be a careful, patient man, who should early learn when to stop work, and his guide should be accuracy first, speed second.

In 1824 Rodman were paid $1 per day including subsistence. Axemen were also paid $1 per day including subsistence. Benjamin Wright, principal engineer in the Eastern section was paid $2,000.00 per month. William Beebe was paid $12.00 plus board per month for unspecified work as a rodman or axeman.

Chaining was not mentioned in this pocket edition, but many persons know this word from reviewing old deeds. One method was the Gunter's chain (Surveyor's chain) which consisted of 100 pieces of steel rods linked together by small rings. The total length of this chain was 66 feet. A link was a smaller measurement with ten links marked by a metal tab representing 0.66 feet or 7.92 inches.

Another useful measurement is 80 chains being equal to one mile. Much of the measurement for the subdivision of public lands in the United States was made with the Gunter's chain. Tapes which are graduated in chains and links are available and are used in connection with modern land surveying.

The following are a few examples of the bench marks located on the Middle Division of the First Enlargement in Camillus, New York.

BM no. 317 - Nine mile creek aqueduct, copper plug, N.W. corner of coping of E. retaining wall, towpath side. Miles from Greenbush 175.98.

BM no. 318 - Culvert no. 58, square cut, N.E. corner of coping, E. wall, first culvert E. of Camillus road bridge, towpath side.

BM no. 319 - Bridge no. 98, Camillus road bridge, copper plug, lower step, W. wing, towpath abutment. not located.

We were always aware that bench marks existed, but we had difficulty locating them prior to the Pocket Book information.

Copper plug - It is interesting to note that a water channel was chiseled in the stone to allow water to flow away from the copper plug - author

The Red line - The red line is a unit of measurement on our abandonment maps denoting the edge or the inner angle of the towpath where it meets the slope wall or a vertical approach wall. Slope walls were angled walls of clay covered with stone riprap to prevent erosion from the canal boat wakes. The State survey of 1901 set round concrete monuments to identify the red line. Concrete monuments were used only for the red line designation.

Left - Red line monument - author - STA 115 OFFSET 5 FT

Rectangular brass plates were inserted onto the top of the concrete base. The red line monuments were placed with a five foot offset from the actual line as it would not be possible to place the monument on the bank or stone edge. This would protect the monuments from towrope wear and the monument would not be subject to erosion.

U.S. Geological Survey bench mark - author

The Blue line - the blue lines are the outermost boundaries denoting canal ownership with the adjacent land owners. Iron rods marked the blue line boundaries. The blue line is the ownership line to the North and South of the canal usually on the far side of the blue line drainage ditch. These ditches paralleled the canal in order to shunt water away from the berme and towpath to avoid erosion and washouts.

"An important policy adopted in 1909 was that of making what are known as "blue line" surveys. On the maps of the original State canals the line showing the boundaries of land acquired by the State for its canals was shown in blue ink. The custom of referring to this as the blue line is now of such long-standing that the term has come to be synonymous with canal land boundary line." History of the Barge Canal of N.Y.S. - Whitford - 1921 p.293.

The State of New York would purchase adjacent lands for buildings, gravel banks, or as their needs dictated, and thus the blue line boundary was widely irregular and varied in width from blue line to blue line.

The U.S. Geological Survey Bench Marks provides another means of checking elevations. A bench mark disc is located on the NE corner of Devoe Road and Thompson Road and was placed in 1953 with an elevation of 442 feet above sea level.

CHAPTER 10

BUILDER'S STONES AND PLAQUES

Many of us look for identification marks, mason symbols, builder's stones or plaques placed on the Erie Canal structures in New York State, but few are in evidence. We have looked extensively on our Nine Mile Creek Aqueduct for any man-made symbols or lettering, but nothing has come into view. There is a bench mark from 1901 as described in the chapter on bench marks. The following descriptions are not an exhaustive study and the readers may know of the location of marks or builder's stones on other structures. I would appreciate being notified of your discoveries.

The closest builder's stone to Camillus is located to the east of Syracuse on Erie Boulevard East. The monument is situated between the east and west bound lanes of Erie Boulevard East, just to the east of Teall Avenue. Lock No. 47 was located to the west of this site. The builder's stone was named after Joseph M. Kasson, the contractor who built Locks No. 47 and 48. The builder's stone is well worn and the last name KASSON and the date 1848 are visible. (see Craig Williams CSNYS guide The Erie Canal DeWitt to New London - 1990)

Monument - 2002 - author

Kasson Builder's Stone - 2002 - author

Plaque - 2002 -author

A plaque is mounted on the south side of the monument which reads as follows:

ALONG THIS ROUTE FOR A CENTURY RAN THE ERIE CANAL
OPENED IN 1825.

THE PRODUCTS OF NEW YORK
STATE'S FIELDS AND FACTORIES
FROM LAKE ERIE TO THE HUDSON
RIVER WERE CARRIED ON IT.

THIS MONUMENT WAS BUILT WITH
STONES OBTAINED FROM VARIOUS
LOCKS THAT WERE LOCATED WITHIN
THE CITY OF SYRACUSE.

ERECTED BY THE DEPARTMENT OF PARKS
AND THE STATE EDUCATION DEPARTMENT.
1935

It is always advisable to ask the local people for help in locating certain structures that may not be readily visible. On a Sunday morning, I was investigating a site very near the monument that was described above. This is usually the best time to search for sites as fewer questions are asked. I was walking back and forth in a used car lot for signs of the twin railroad tunnels that carried the New York Central under the canal near Teall Avenue. I had a clip board in one hand and a map in the other. I saw a rather large man built like a tree, approaching me after about 30 minutes on the site. He came directly up to me and demanded in a loud voice, "What are you doing on my property?" He had observed me from the coffee shop across the road. There was a pause on my part. I explained hurriedly who I was (which meant nothing), and what I was looking for. There was a pause again. He looked down at me and smiled and said, "Oh yes, I'll show you where that is!" My heart started again!

DURHAMVILLE CULVERT This culvert has undergone a long series of rebuilding. In Whitford, Vol. 1, p. 1110, the Durhamville structure is listed as a spillway with 6 gates with steel as the material in the bulkhead. It is located between Locks 46 (Utica) and 47 (Syracuse).

The contractor of record was Pierce and Story. The builders stone is now part of the rip-wrap on the east end of the spillway.

Builder's Stone Pierce and Story 1840 - photo taken in 1991 - stone removed from structure and now used as riprap - author

OTIS EDDY - BUILDER 1841 - taken 1990 by author - The aqueduct towpath and prism are now closed due to safety consideration.

SCHOHARIE AQUEDUCT The Schoharie Creek Aqueduct was listed as No. 5 on the First Enlargement with a total length of 624 feet 3 inches. There is a builder's stone mounted in the middle of the Aqueduct dedicated to Otis Eddy. It reads as follows:

Builder's Stone - Yankee Hill First Enlargement Lock No. 28.

Lock No. 28
Arch C. Powell Res. Eng. (Resident Engineer)
William Coleman & Co. Contractor
1841
Photo taken in 1991 by author

The Aqueduct was completed in 1844. Efforts to stabilize the structure have been going on for many years. Cables were used to hold the end of the Aqueduct where earlier piers were removed. There was a major collapse of the last pier and arch in 2002 due to several causes, but the most obvious is the dropping of the water level in Schoharie Creek. Cables were inserted to hold the disconnected end arch in place, but corrosion have caused the cables to brake.

Medina Road Culvert Dedication Stones

This is the only road culvert that allowed vehicles to go under the original Clinton's Ditch, the First Enlargement and the present Erie section of the Barge Canal. This is listed in "Believe it or Not" by Ripley. The culvert went under the three canals and was lengthened and the south portal was rebuilt each time. The road culvert under the first enlargement was described in Whitford, Vol. 1, p. 1097 as an arch 162 feet 6 inches in length with a span, or width of 19 feet and a height of 13 feet. It was made entirely of stone. There were two cornerstones at the culvert. The one cornerstone is located in the foundation of the home of Vernon Toussaint on the south west side of the south portal on Culvert Road.

Medina Road Culvert South Portal

Toussant Corner Stone - 1990 - by author

PRINCIPAL ENGINEER
DAVID THOMAS
OGDEN MALLORY
Builder
WM. E. PERINE
SAMUEL B. COLLIN
JOHN DRAKE (Le) ?
Contractor
D. 1823

Cornerstone - 1998 - autho. The cornerstone reads as follows:

CANAL COMMISSIONERS
DEWITT CLINTON President of the Board
STEPHEN VAN RENSSELAER
MYRON HOLLEY
SAMUEL YOUNG
HENRY SEYMOUR
WM. C. BOUCK
D. 1823

The second cornerstone is the property of the Canal Society of New York State and is located at the Camillus Erie Canal Park and Sims' Store Museum. Richard Wright was the founder of the Onondaga Historical Society and the CSNYS. He had heard that the cornerstone had been removed from the Medina site and moved to a historical society in Oswego, N.Y. Richard Wright felt that this should be the property of the CSNYS, and he went to Oswego and returned with the cornerstone. It was placed in the foyer of 311 Montgomery Street where it remained for many years. OHA called us and said they wanted the stone removed along with the sign from the Port Byron Erie House. Four of us went to the OHA to remove the stone and bring it to Camillus for safe keeping. The stone must weigh at least 1000 pounds. The four of us managed to slide the stone down the outside stairs and onto the sidewalk by using boards. The stone was so heavy, the four of us were unable to lift or slide the stone onto a pick-up truck. The curator said that she had an idea. She went across the street into the YMCA and came back with two weight lifters. The six of us lifted and pushed the corner stone onto the truck, and it is exhibited at our Camillus Erie Canal Park and Sims' Store Museum.

We had an interesting incident while in Durhamville. Ten years ago I canoed on the Erie Canal First Enlargement from the Dewitt, N.Y. widewaters near the Butternut Creek Aqueduct, to New London, New York. New London is where the present Barge Canal, Erie section, cut through the Erie Canal First Enlargement. The old canal basically is a source of water for the Barge Canal.

My wife, Liz, dropped me off in Dewitt and was going to pick-me up in New London two and a half days later. Cell phones were not invented as yet, to any degree. The entire 30 mile section did not allow camping as it is considered a State park. The towpath was patrolled by motorbikes, and they went home at 5 PM. I tented about 7 PM in an area that was semi-wild and not visible from the roads.

In Canastota, N.Y., I had to portage through the business section of town with my 17 foot canoe. I had constructed a clamp-on single wheel for the bow of the canoe and wheeled the canoe through downtown Canastota at high noon. The street light changed while I was in the intersection, and no one honked or yelled at me. Several men offered to help.

The challenge arrived when I crossed over the Durhamville Enlarged Erie Oneida Creek Culvert and Waste Weir. I encountered two corrugated drainage culverts under Route 46. It was extremely dangerous to cross the highway with a canoe on my head. I chose to enter one of the culvert pipes. While lying on my back and using a short handled paddle against the rounded culvert pipe ceiling, I was able to propel myself forward. The tolerance was very close. If I became stuck on a log, I could hopefully reverse my direction or slide out of the canoe into the water in the culvert and walk out the way I entered. Thousands of hanging spiders climbed up their webs into the corrugations at the top of the culvert pipe. Not one of the spiders dropped into the canoe. I emerged on the east side and headed for New London, N.Y., where Liz arrived at our designated location.

Chapter 11

Buoy Boat

We were very fortunate to obtain a Barge Canal buoy boat in the year 2001. I had remembered that a buoy boat existed and was housed in the closed Cedar Bay Museum in Dewitt, N.Y., which was an extension of the Erie Canal Museum in downtown Syracuse. Andy Kitzman, acting director at that time, expressed interest in releasing the buoy boat to our Camillus Erie Canal Park. Buoy boats cannot be purchased, but can be leased on a long term basis from the Canal Corporation.

Cedar Bay built the museum around the buoy boat. The boat was placed on a wooden platform and the floor was poured around the boat. The cement was removed around the protective skid around the propeller and rudder. We obviously did not want to remove one wall of the building in order to retrieve the boat. The Canal Museum was not thrilled with the idea either. Bill Winks of our Camillus Highway Department, designed and constructed a split axle under the bow of the boat so that the boat could be moved out of the door. A regular axle would raise the boat too high from the floor and the boat would not clear the top of the garage door. A normal height axle was placed under the stern of the boat. There was no more than one inch to spare when the boat cleared the doorway and was placed onto a low-boy trailer for its trip to Camillus.

On trailer

The canal buoy boat no. 126 is a static display for educational and historical purposes. The number of the buoy boat is officially no. 126, but the number was changed at some time and the number no. 159 now appears on the boat. The late John Zmarthie of the NYS Canal Corporation made this transfer possible.

Many of the buoy boats were made at the Syracuse Barge Canal Terminal and Shop. "Twelve new buoy boats were built in 1931 to replace the equal number condemned. The steel buoy boats are all electric welded. " Two 27 feet welded steel buoy boats, no. 155 and no. 156, were constructed in 1939."

Craig Williams sent me a copy of the original building specifications for Buoy Boat no. 126.

Length - 28 ft. Beam - 7 ft. Depth - 3 ft. 7 in.
Year Built - 1930
Acquired by State - 1930
Cost - $1800
Reconditioned - 1953
Engine - Lathrop - gas - 30 H.P. - 3 cylinders
Approx. fuel consumption - 3 gals. per hour - 15 gals. per day
Loaned to Syracuse Museum on permit in 1958
General equipment - 1 fire extinguisher - 1 pike pole - 1 bow and 1 port light.
One 25 foot bow line - one 25 foot stern line - one starting crank

The following details of a buoy boat in operation were obtained from Dan Geist, retired with the DOT and the Canal Corporation of New York State. The buoy boat serviced the kerosene lanterns that marked the channels on the Barge Canal for night passage. One man was responsible to service about 30 lanterns in a day. He would go against the current and into the wind to contact the buoy , then leave the pilot house and loosely tie the boat to the buoy.

The buoy boat operator, before beginning his daily routine, would have 10 lanterns serviced and ready to exchange with the canal lanterns that either had blown-out or had run out of kerosene. After the exchange, the captain would stop and refill the next 10 lanterns with kerosene, trim the wicks or replace them and clean the globes. Due to the large reservoir at their base, lanterns could, depending on the wind conditions, burn for a period of a few weeks. On an average, Dan would run about 10-15 miles on a buoy run.

The frame or bale holding the lantern was bolted to the buoy so it could be replaced easily in case it was damaged. Two clips held the lantern on the sides and a spring clip was attached on the top ring of the lantern. This spring prevented jarring of the lantern due to wind or a passing boat wake. Strong winds or vandals shooting out the glass globes could put out the flame. Swimmers would also tip the buoys over, and flood the glass lantern dome. In approximately 1969, electric battery lit lamps were used, but proved unsatisfactory.

For a short period of time during the winter months the buoy boats were stored in boat houses. Wooden deck covers were used. Buoy tenders originally purchased their

Lantern on Buoy - file photo, NYS archives

Lantern - State Museum, Albany
- author

own boats, but later the state provided them. Wooden boats were gradually replaced with steel hulls in the 1930's. A sweepboat was pushed by a buoy boat to check the depth of the canal each spring. Thank you very much Dan for this insight on how buoys were maintained.

Buoy Boat 141, Lyons, N.Y. - author

Buoy Boat 159 on stand in Camillus - author

Buoy Boat 159 on trailer - S. Settineri

State buoy boat at Inner Harbor, Syracuse - author

Chapter 12

OLYMPIC TORCH

We received a phone call from the Olympic Committee in early January, 1996. They wanted the Olympic Torch to be carried by different modes of transportation on its journey throughout the United States, ending at Atlanta, Georgia, the site of the Olympics. The chairman asked us to provide a mule drawn canal boat to transport the torch from our Sims' Museum on Devoe Road to the earthen dam located at the aqueduct, one mile to the east. We quickly and emphatically answered, "Yes, we will provide what is needed!" We then realized that we did not have a canal boat or mules. This was just a minor challenge.

We had another problem to overcome. There were about 35 trees remaining along the towpath that would prevent the mules from pulling the boat with a towline. Many of the trees were leaning toward the canal, and later we found that about 15 trees had dryrot within. We felt that there was a safety issue with our boats filled with children and patrons passing under the trees each day. We had the trees cut down and brought to an open area near our equipment shed. We hired a man with a portable saw mill to cut the trees into usable boards. We used these boards to build the superstructure on a discarded steel hull stern paddle wheeler that John Settineri obtained. Before the scrapped steel shell could be used , it needed minor repairs and the entire boat crew worked that spring to scrape , clean and paint the hull. We built a wooden deck and stern cabin, and the final product looked like a first enlargement hurry-up rescue boat. We did not have time to properly cure the lumber for use on the boat. It was quite green and warped at the time the torch arrived. We named it the Wentworth - Bunce Freight Company after two of our long time volunteers.

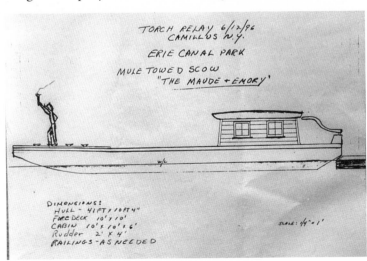

Sketch of Camillus built Olympic Torch boat - John Settineri

Building boat

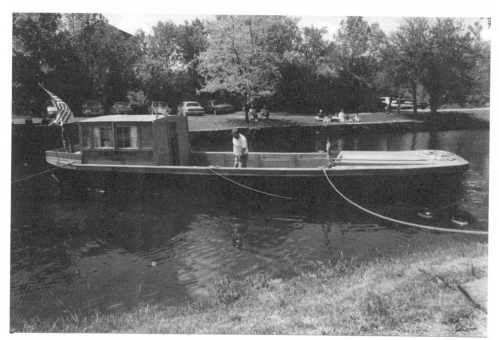

Launching Olympic Torch boat

Practice sessions - John Luebs - The date was June 12, 1996.

The Town of Camillus Police Department planned and coordinated the communications and the crowd control. The police estimated the crowd at Sims' Museum to be about 10,000 . There were many additional people along the route and more waiting at the aqueduct.

I asked a young man from the Civil Air Patrol to save several seats in the front of the viewing stand until the boat left the dock. My wife, Liz, arrived with several elderly ladies and asked to use the seats that were being saved. The young man dutifully stated that Dr. Beebe said to save the seats at all cost. Liz calmly said that was commendable. She was Mrs. Beebe, and I outrank Dr. Beebe, and we are going to use these seats! Thank you.

John Settineri asked Mike Milewski from the Rome Erie Canal Village if he would be available to use their mules to pull our new canal boat. Mike was happy to oblige. We had several practice sessions using the mules. We tried successfully to keep the people away from the towpath to protect the mules from being spooked.

The convoy with the Torch arrived at dusk and the young lady carried the torch to the dock for a brief ceremony before boarding the boat. When the signal was given, the towline tightened and the Wentworth and Bunce started its torch carrying journey to the east. Due to the noise and excitement, the mules traveled fairly rapidly. As we approached the end point at the earthen dam dock, slowing down of the boat posed a problem. Bill Winks jumped off, and as he sank into the mud, he pushed against the bow to slow the boat . The torch was passed to another runner and the torch bearer, with escorting motor scooters, disappeared to the east into darkness.

Olympic Torch Boat at dock in front of Sims' Museum - John Luebs

Olympic Torch Boat at dock.

Torch on boat at start of boat run

One of our volunteers on traffic detail, stopped a car and related that the road was closed to all traffic. After the explanation, the driver said thank you, and mentioned that he was the Camillus Chief of Police, Lloyd Perkins.

It took many volunteers in a short period of time to accomplish an extremely difficult task. In the case of the Olympic Torch, the volunteers spent about six months preparing for its arrival, and the actual procession lasted less than 30 minutes.

Olympic Torch bearer at dock in front of Sims' Museum - author

About the Author

For 35 years I have been the volunteer director of the Town of Camillus Erie Canal Park and Sims' Store Museum. Under my direction, the Camillus Erie Canal Park has grown from the original 164 acres to 420. Over 120 active trained volunteers manage and operate the seven mile lineal water-filled canal. We provide extensive school programs, narrated boat rides on the historical canal for Sunday visitors, dinner cruises and tours for many diverse groups. We develop and construct the many canal exhibits within Sims' Store Museum, outside buildings and static displays.

We have placed the 1844 Nine Mile Creek Aqueduct on the National Registry of Historical Places, and we will be going to bid for its reconstruction. We have worked closely with Craig Williams of the New York State Museum in Albany in researching the many unique canal structures located in our park.

For the past 20 years, I have been an active member of the Board of Directors of the Canal Society New York State, serving on the ad hoc committee to establish an historical Erie Canal Site at Port Byron in conjunction with the Thruway Authority. At the 2000 World Canal Conference in Rochester, New York, as a guest lecturer, my wife and I received "The Spirit of the Canal Award". We have visited and studied the canals of Northern and Southern France, as well as the Waterways of Britain.

Locally, I enjoy lecturing, leading field trips to local canal sites and the Camillus Unique Forest Area and presenting programs to civic, library and historical organizations. For more than 10 years I have been one of the directors of the Nine Mile Creek Conservation Council which has developed a water trail along Nine Mile Creek. This group was also responsible for saving and creating the Camillus Unique Forest Area.

Now that I have retired from 44 years of dental practice, I look forward to the daily discoveries at the Camillus Erie Canal Park and surrounding sites.